SIGNS: AN INTRODUCTION TO SEMIOTICS

Second Edition

From the simplest hand gesture to the most complex diagram or chart, the sign is the key to the communication of ideas. In this book, Thomas A. Sebeok examines, in an engaging, readable style, how the sign mediates between bodily experience and abstract thought. Semiosis is the instinctive capacity of all organisms to produce and understand signs, and semiotics, the study of signs, offers powerful analytical tools for application to the study of perception. In this regard, semiotics is of relevance to a wide spectrum of scholars and professionals, including social scientists, psychologists, artists, graphic designers, and students of literature.

This second edition of *Signs* combines some of Sebeok's most important essays with a new general introduction, a glossary, and a revised and expanded bibliography and index. From an overview of the discipline to a more detailed exploration of sign categories, the author demonstrates the interconnection between verbal and nonverbal communication.

Aimed primarily at undergraduate and graduate students, this book will also be of interest to anyone who is interested in exploring and analysing the complex sign systems we so often take for granted.

(Toronto Studies in Semiotics and Communication)

THOMAS A. SEBEOK is Distinguished Professor Emeritus of Linguistics and Semiotics at Indiana University. He has written numerous articles and books, and is world-renowned as an authority on semiotics.

THOMAS A. SEBEOK

Signs: An Introduction to Semiotics

Second Edition

UNIVERSITY OF TORONTO PRESS
Toronto Buffalo London

© University of Toronto Press Incorporated
First Edition 1994, reprinted 1999
Second Edition 2001

Toronto Buffalo London
Printed in Canada

ISBN 0-8020-3634-1 (cloth)
ISBN 0-8020-8472-9 (paper)

∞

Print on acid-free paper

Toronto Studies in Semiotics and Communication
Editors: Marcel Danesi, Umberto Eco, Paul Perron, Peter Schultz,
Thomas A. Sebeok

National Library of Canada Cataloguing in Publication Data

Sebeok, Thomas A., 1920–
   Signs : an introduction to semiotics

   2nd ed.
   (Toronto studies in semiotics and communication)
   Includes bibliographical references and index.
   ISBN 0-8020-3634-1 (bound)   ISBN 0-8020-8472-9 (pbk.)

   1. Semiotics.   2. Signs and symbols.   I. Title.   II. Series.

   P99.S38 2001   302.2   C2001-901772-3

University of Toronto Press acknowledges the financial assistance to   its publishing program of the Canada Council for the Arts and the Ontario Arts
Council.

University of Toronto Press acknowledges the financial support for its publishing activities of the Government of Canada through the Book Publishing
Industry Development Program (BPIDP).

Contents

Preface to the Second Edition

This second edition of *Signs* includes several features that are designed to make it more comprehensive and useful as an introductory manual for semiotics. The original eight chapters have remained virtually intact, with minor modifications here and there. As mentioned in the first edition, these were reworkings of studies that have appeared in the following sources: chapter 2 in the *Journal of Social and Biological Structures*; chapter 3 in *Semiotica*; chapter 4 in *New Directions in Linguistics and Semiotics*, edited by James E. Copeland (Houston: Rice University Studies); chapters 5 and 7 in the *American Journal of Semiotics*; chapter 6 in *Modern Language Notes*; chapter 8 in the *Georgetown University Round Table Monographs*; and chapter 9 in *The Semiotics of Culture*, edited by Henri Broms and Rebecca Kaufman (Helsinki: Arator, 1988).

Chapter 1 is new to this edition. It is a reworking of a lecture entitled 'Nonverbal Communication,' which appeared in the *Thomas A. Sebeok Distinguished Lecture Series in Semiotics*, Vol. 1 (2000), initially published by the Program in Semiotics and Communication Theory of Victoria College, in collaboration with University College, University of Toronto. The series is edited and introduced by Marcel Danesi and Paul Perron. It presents in a general way some of the basic notions that are used in the remainder of the book.

This second edition also contains a glossary of technical terms and an expanded bibliography, as well as a thoroughly reworked index. These features are intended to augment its textbook functions.

Thomas A. Sebeok
Indiana University, 2001

Foreword:
Thomas A. Sebeok and Semiotics

MARCEL DANESI

The name of Thomas A. Sebeok is universally associated with the development of semiotics and communication theory in the twentieth century. Indeed, no one else in the world today has had the enormous impact that Professor Sebeok has had on these two fields. It would be no exaggeration to say that without his innovative research and his critical writings, both fields would not be as flourishing and as significant as they are today, as we the start the new millennium.

It was appropriate in 1992 to launch the Toronto Studies in Semiotics series with Professor Sebeok's introductory manual to the science of semiotics. It is befitting to inaugurate the expansion of the series – now renamed the Toronto Studies in Semiotics and Communication – with the second edition of *Signs*. In his numerous ground-breaking works, there is a constant reminder by Professor Sebeok, in fact, that communication is grounded in the semiosic system of the organism. One cannot be studied independently of the other.

This second edition, like the first one, has both theoretical and practical value. It can be used as a theoretical framework for studying sign-based phenomena in semiotics, communication theory, psychology, linguistics, and biology. It can also be used as a textbook in advanced university courses in these disciplinary domains. Professor Sebeok's writing is lucid, yet challenging. He has the exceptional talent of being able to explain a difficult topic to a large audience, simply yet with technical skill and great erudition.

No wonder, then, that the first edition of the present work became a contemporary classic in the field shortly after its publication. His writing is simultaneously entertaining and thought-provoking; usable by student and scholar alike.

It is not commonly known that the science of signs, *semiotics*, grew out of attempts by the first physicians of the Western world to understand how the interaction between the body and the mind operates within specific cultural domains. Indeed, in its oldest usage, the term *semiotics* was applied to the study of the observable pattern of physiological symptoms induced by particular diseases. Hippocrates (460?–377? B.C.) – the founder of medical science – viewed the ways in which an individual in a specific culture would manifest and relate the symptomatology associated with a disease as the basis upon which to carry out an appropriate diagnosis and then to formulate a suitable prognosis. The physician Galen of Pergamum (A.D. 130?–200?) similarly referred to diagnosis as a process of semiosis. It was soon after Hippocrates' utilization of the term *semeiosis* to refer to the cultural representation of symptomatic signs that it came to mean, by the time of Aristotle (384–322 B.C.), the 'reference system' of a sign itself.

So, from the dawn of civilization to the present age, it has always been recognized in Western culture – at least implicitly – that there is an intrinsic connection between the body, the mind, and culture, and that the process that interlinks these three dimensions of human existence is *semiosis*, the production and interpretation of signs. The *raison d'être* of semiotics is, arguably, to investigate the interconnection between life and semiosis. And that is what Sebeok has taught a whole generation of semioticians. His interlinked series of books published over three decades, from 1976 to 2001 – *Contributions to the Doctrine of Signs* (1976), *The Sign and Its Masters* (1979), *The Play of Musement* (1981), *I Think I Am a Verb* (1986), *A Sign Is Just a Sign* (1991), *Semiotics in the United States* (1991), *The Forms of Meaning* (2000, with M. Danesi), and *Global Semiotics* (2001) – have shown how semiosis interacts with biological, psychological, and cultural processes and products. This book has been designed as a synthesis of his research on the 'elemental' features of this interaction. It gathers some of his most important essays dealing with the fundamental issues of contemporary semiotic theory and practice. These have been reworked into a cohesive textbook that is usable by semiotician, student of semiotics and communication theory, cognitive scientist, linguist, psychologist, philosopher, and general reader alike.

The opening chapter ('Basic Notions') is new to the second edition. It presents in a clear and illustrated style the basic concepts of semiotic analysis. The second chapter ('The Study of Signs') constitutes an overview of the intriguing study of human semiosis, including a delimitation of the scientific field of semiotics. The third chapter ('Six Species of Signs') delineates and illustrates the six fundamental categories of signs – signal, symptom, icon, index, symbol, name. What becomes clear from this chapter is that semiosis is *the* defining characteristic of biological life. Then, in chapter four ('Symptom Signs'), Sebeok focuses on the nature of symptoms. It is instructive to note that the analysis of the body's genetically programmed system of symptoms that indicate patterns of disease in the ancient world laid the foundation for the science of signs. The act of interpreting symptoms constitutes the essence of semiosic analysis. A symptom stands for some malfunction or 'interrupted' bodily process which, in the mind of the physician, points to, or 'represents,' a disease, ailment, or malady. In chapter five ('Indexical Signs') Sebeok then examines what is arguably the most fundamental category of 'conscious' signing – indexicality. In human semiosis, this inheres in the process of pointing out the objects, events, and beings in the world. Indexicality can manifest itself in sign tokens that range all the way from the pointing action of the index finger to the use of words such as *here* and *there*. In the sixth chapter ('Iconic Signs'), Sebeok then examines the nature of iconicity, the signifying process by which a sign represents its referent by simulating one or all of its physical (or noetical) properties. Utilizing a broad range of examples from Nature, Sebeok's treatment drives home the point that iconicity constitutes a central principle of semiosic organization and patterning in all life forms. Then in the seventh chapter ('Fetish Signs'), Sebeok takes a delightful excursion into an area that clearly illustrates the nature of 'symbolic semiosis' in humans – fetish signs. Although fetishism

is found in primates and mammals, it is a phenomenon that
saliently illustrates how semiosis interconnects biological, psychological, and cultural processes in the human species. The fetish is a
microcosm of what we are – consumers of symbols. In chapter
eight ('Language Signs') Sebeok then brings us into the exclusively human domain of verbal semiosis. Language is the ultimate
achievement of the body-mind-culture transformational semiosic
process. But, as he cogently reminds us, it is not always a superior
one to the nonverbal mode of knowing and signing. Human communication must be thought of in its totality – as a verbal *and* nonverbal process. Finally, in the last chapter ('Language as a Primary
Modelling System?'), Sebeok provides us with one of the clearest
and most plausible accounts of the origin and evolution of language in the human species. Language, for Sebeok, is an effective
cognitive means for modelling the world. It developed to allow
humans to portray the world around them in an efficient way.
'Speech,' or articulated language, is a derivative of this modelling
capacity; it is, to use a recently coined biological term, an 'exaptation' from the language capacity. In essence, Sebeok argues that
nonverbal signing is more fundamental to survival, both phylogenetically and ontogenetically, than is verbal signing.

It is difficult indeed to formulate a single theme as characteristic
of these intellectually fascinating pages, other than the idea that
semiosis is life. Sebeok's treatment documents the manifestations
of semiosis in vastly different species (from termites to humans),
and leads us to conclude that the ability to manufacture signs is a
basic survival strategy in all life forms. In humans the persistence
of the iconic mode of thought suggests that concepts start out as
mimetic or osmotic portrayals of the physical environment. These
are at first tied to the operations of our sensory apparatus. It is only
after they have become routinized through cultural diffusion that
they become free of sensory control and take on an abstract quality. For Sebeok, iconicity lies at the core of how the human organism responds to the world.

Like the great biologist Jakob von Uexküll (1864–1944) – whose
'discovery' by North American scientists is due in large part to
Sebeok's efforts – Sebeok finds a point of contact between a main-

stream scientific approach to the study of organisms – *biology* – and that of the strictly *semiotic* tradition. J. von Uexküll argued that every organism had different inward and outward 'lives.' The key to understanding this duality is in the anatomical structure of the organism itself. Animals with widely divergent anatomies do not live in the same kind of world. There exists, therefore, no common world of referents shared by humans and animals equally. The work of von Uexküll and Sebeok has shown that an organism does not perceive an object in itself, but according to its own particular kind of pre-existent mental modelling system that allows it to interpret the world of beings, objects, and events in a biologically-programmed way. For Sebeok, this system is grounded in the organism's body, which routinely converts the external world of experience into an internal one of representation in terms of the particular features of the *modelling system* with which a specific species is endowed.

Sebeok has transformed semiotics back into a 'life science,' having relocated it, in effect, to its roots in medical biology. In other words, he has uprooted semiotics from the philosophical, linguistic, and hermeneutic terrain in which it has been cultivated for centuries and replanted it in the larger biological domain whence it sprang originally. Sebeok's biological approach inheres in a perspective that aims to investigate how all animals are endowed genetically with the capacity to use basic signals and signs for survival, and how human semiosis is both similar to, and different from, this capacity. He distils rudimentary elements of semiosis from animate reality so as to establish a taxonomy of notions, principles, and procedures for understanding the uniqueness of human semiosis. The result is a program for studying human knowing as a biological capacity that transforms sensory-based and affectively motivated responses into a world of mental models. Signs are forged within the human organism as extensions of the body's response system. No matter how bizarre or unearthly the shape of creatures which might inhabit alien planets, we are likely to recognize them as animals nonetheless. The chief basis for this recognition is that they are bound to give off 'signs of life.'

There is no doubt in my mind that the reader will find Sebeok, in comparison to other major figures in the field of semiotics, quite enjoyable to read. But underlying his masterful ability to convey a sense of enjoyment is a deep understanding of semiosis. Indeed, in having transformed the mainstream study of semiosis into a life science, Sebeok has greatly expanded the nature of semiotic inquiry and attracted, in the process, more and more interest in it from the behavioural, cognitive, and social sciences. As he argues throughout the pages of this book, a biologically based semiotics will allow us to get a glimpse into how the body interacts with the mind to produce signs, messages, thought, and, ultimately, cultural behaviour.

This book is intended to be both a synthetic overview of (bio)semiotics and a compendium of practical illustrations showing how that discipline can inform and potentially expand the method of inquiry in both semiotics and biology. Each chapter contains numerous practical exemplifications and insights into the potential applications of semiotics to the study of cross-species modelling. Nevertheless, the writing is not so diluted as to make it an overly simplified treatment. Some effort to understand the contents of each chapter on the part of the reader will be required. The more technical parts might entail several rereadings. For the sake of comprehensiveness, I have appended at the back an extensive bibliography of works upon which the Sebeokian framework has been built, as well as a convenient glossary of technical terms.

Victoria College,
University of Toronto, 2001

SIGNS: AN INTRODUCTION TO SEMIOTICS

Second Edition

1

Basic Notions

The phenomenon that distinguishes life forms from inanimate objects is *semiosis*. This can be defined simply as the instinctive capacity of all living organisms to produce and understand *signs*.

A sign is any physical *form* that has been imagined or made externally (through some physical medium) to stand for an object, event, feeling, etc., known as a *referent*, or for a class of similar (or related) objects, events, feelings, etc., known as a *referential domain*. In human life, signs serve many functions. They allow people to recognize patterns in things; they act as predictive guides or plans for taking actions; they serve as exemplars of specific kinds of phenomena; and the list could go on and on. The English word *cat*, for example, is an example of a particular kind of human sign – known as *verbal* – which stands for a referent that can be described as a 'carnivorous mammal with a tail, whiskers, and retractile claws.'

Each species produces and understands certain kinds of specific signs for which it has been programmed by its biology. These can range from simple bodily signals to advanced symbolic structures such as words. Signs allow each species to (1) signal its existence, (2) communicate messages within the species, and (3) model incoming information from the external world. *Semiotics* is the science that studies these functions. The goal of this opening chapter is to introduce several basic notions for the formal study of semiosis.

The Object of Semiotics

Semiotics arose from the scientific study of the physiological symptoms induced by particular diseases or physical states. It was Hippocrates (460–377 B.C.), the founder of Western medical science, who
established *semeiotics* as a branch of medicine for the study of *symptoms* – a *symptom* being, in effect, a *sēmeion* 'mark, sign' that stands for
something other than itself. The physician's primary task, Hippocrates claimed, was to unravel what a symptom stands for. For example, a dark bruise, a rash, or a sore throat might stand respectively
for a broken finger, a skin allergy, a cold. The medical problem is, of
course, to infer what that *something* is. Medical diagnosis is, in effect,
semiotic science, since it is based on the principle that the physical
symptom stands not for itself but for an inner state or condition.
The physician Galen of Pergamum (A.D. 139–199) further en-
trenched *semeiotics* into medical practice several centuries later.

The study of signs in non-medical terms became the target of philosophers around the time of Aristotle (384–322 B.C.) and the Stoic
philosophers. Aristotle defined the sign as consisting of three
dimensions: (1) the physical part of the sign itself (e.g., the sounds
that make up the word *cat*); (2) the *referent* to which it calls attention
(a certain category of feline mammal); and (3) its evocation of a
meaning (what the referent entails psychologically and socially).
These three dimensions are simultaneous: i.e., it is impossible
to think of a word such as *cat* (a vocal sign made up of the sounds
c-a-t), without thinking at the same time of the type of mammal
to which it refers (the feline mammal), and without experiencing
the personal and social meaning(s) that such a referent entails.

The next major step forward in the study of signs was the one
taken by St Augustine (A.D. 354–430), the philosopher and religious
thinker who was among the first to distinguish clearly between *natural* (symptoms, animal signals, etc.) and *conventional* (human-
made) signs, and to espouse the view that there is an inbuilt *interpre-
tive* component to the whole process of representation. John Locke
(1632–1704), the English philosopher who set out the principles of
empiricism, introduced the formal study of signs into philosophy in
his *Essay Concerning Human Understanding* (1690), anticipating that
it would allow philosophers to understand the interconnection

between representation and knowledge. But the task he laid out remained virtually unnoticed until the ideas of the Swiss linguist Ferdinand de Saussure (1857–1913) and the American philosopher Charles S. Peirce (1839–1914) became the basis for circumscribing an autonomous field of inquiry which sought to understand the *structures* that undergird both the production and interpretation of signs. The premise that guides structuralist semiotics is, in fact, that the recurring patterns that characterize sign systems are reflective of innate *structures* in the sensory, emotional, and intellectual composition of the human body and the human psyche. This would explain why the forms of expression that humans create and to which they respond instinctively the world over are so meaningful and so easily understandable across cultures. In his *Cours de linguistique générale* (1916), a textbook put together after his death by two of his university students, Saussure used the term *semiology* to designate the field he proposed for studying these structures. But while his term is still used somewhat today, the older term *semiotics* is the preferred one. Saussure emphasized that the study of signs should be divided into two branches – the *synchronic* and the *diachronic*. The former refers to the study of signs at a given point in time, normally the present, and the latter to the investigation of how signs change in form and meaning over time.

Semiotics is both a *science*, with its own corpus of findings and its theories, and a *technique* for studying anything that produces signs. This is why Charles Peirce defined semiotics, as did the philosopher John Locke before him, as the 'doctrine' of signs (Peirce 1958/2: 228). The word *doctrine* was not used by Peirce in its religious sense, but rather in its basic meaning of 'system of principles.' In subsequent chapters, we will encounter many of the modern-day founders of the theory of signs. Suffice it to say here that all have worked under the frameworks developed by Saussure and Peirce.

Defining the Sign

Saussure's definition of the sign laid down the course that semiotic inquiry was to take during the first half of the twentieth century. He defined it as a form made up (1) of something physical –

sounds, letters, gestures, etc. – which he termed the *signifier*; and (2) of the image or concept to which the signifier refers – which he called the *signified*. He then called the relation that holds between the two *signification*. Saussure considered the connection between the signifier and the signified an arbitrary one that human beings and/or societies have established at will. To make his point, he reasoned that there was no evident reason for using, say, *tree* or *arbre* (French) to designate 'an arboreal plant.' Indeed, any well-formed signifier could have been used in either language – a well-formed signifier is one that is consistent with the orthographic, phonological, or other type of structure characteristic of the code to which it appertains (*tree* is well formed in English; *tbky* is not).

Peirce called the signifier a *representamen* (literally 'something that does the representing'), a form inhering in the physical strategy of representation itself (the use of sounds, hand movements, etc. for some referential purpose). Peirce termed the referent the *object*, an entity displaced from its (real-world) context of occurrence. He termed the meaning that one gets from a sign the *interpretant*, suggesting that it entailed a form of 'negotiation,' so to speak, whereby the sign-user evaluates or responds to what the sign means socially, contextually, personally, etc.

Structural Properties

Signs of all types are recognizable as such because they have certain predictable and regular properties or *structures*. For example, most human signs have the capacity to encode two primary kinds of referents, *denotative* and *connotative*, depending on usage and situation. *Denotation* is the initial referent a sign *intends* to capture. But the *denoted referent*, or *denotatum*, is not something specific in the world, but rather a prototypical *category* of something. For instance, the word *cat* does not refer to a specific 'cat,' although it can, but to the *category* of animals that we recognize as having the quality 'catness.' The denotative meaning of *cat* is, therefore, really *catness*, a prototypical mental picture marked by specific *distinctive features* such as [mammal], [retractile claws], [long tail], etc. This composite mental picture allows us to determine if a specific real or imaginary animal under consideration will fall within the category of *catness*. Now, in human semiosis a sign can be *extended* freely to encompass other kinds of referents that appear, by association or analogy, to have something in common with the denotatum. This *extensional* process is known as *connotation*, and the new referents are known as *connotata*. Consider the use of the word *cat* in the following two sentences: (1) 'He's a cool *cat* (person who appears to have favourable feline qualities)'; and (2) 'The *cat* is out of the bag (in reference to a secret being revealed). Note that the original referent is implicit in such extensional uses. Any connotative extension of the word *cat* is thus constrained by the distinctive features of the referent.

Such distinctions of meaning crystallize through the inbuilt property of signs known as *paradigmaticity*. Consider the following word pairs: (1) *pin-bin*, (2) *fun-pun*, (3) *duck-luck*. The initial sound of each pair is different and sufficient to indicate a difference in reference. This differentiation feature of signs is known as *paradigmatic* structure – i.e., the relation whereby some minimal feature in a sign is sufficient to keep it differentiated from all other signs of the same kind. Now, note that the above words are legitimate signs, not only because they are differentiable in a specific way, but also because the combination of sounds with which they are constructed is consistent with English syllable structure. On the other hand, *tpin, tbin, tfun, tpun, tduck*, and *tluck* would not be legitimate signs in English because they violate its syllable structure. Syllable structure is known technically as *syntagmatic* structure – i.e., the relation whereby signs are constructed in some definable sequence or combination.

Messages can be constructed on the basis of single signs or, more often than not, as combinations of them. The latter are known as *texts*. A *text* constitutes, in effect, a specific 'weaving together' of signs in order to communicate something. The signs that go into the make-up of texts belong to specific *codes*. These can be defined as systems of signs that are held together by paradigmatic and syntagmatic relations. Cartesian geometry, for instance, is a *code* because it has specific kinds of structural properties. Now, this code can be used to make certain kinds of *texts*: e.g., maps with latitude and longitude lines, certain city designs (as for downtown

Manhattan), and so on. Language too is a code because it has paradigmatic (*pin* vs *bin*) and syntagmatic (*plan* but not *pfan*) properties. Needless to say, it also can be used to make certain kinds of *texts*: e.g., conversations, novels, poems, etc.

Clearly, a text bears no meaning unless the receiver of the text knows the code(s) from which it was constructed and unless the text refers to, occurs in, or entails some specific *context*. The *context* is the environment – physical, psychological, and social – in which a sign or text is used or occurs.

Semiosis and Representation

The primary objective of semiotics is to understand both a species' capacity to make and understand signs and, in the case of the human species, the knowledge-making *activity* this capacity allows human beings to carry out. The former is known, as mentioned above, as *semiosis*, while the latter activity is known as *representation*. Representation is a deliberate use of signs to probe, classify, and hence *know* the world. *Semiosis* is the biological capacity itself that underlies the production and comprehension of signs, from simple physiological signals to those that reveal a highly complex symbolism.

Human intellectual and social life is based on the production, use, and exchange of signs and representations. When we gesture, talk, write, read, watch a TV program, listen to music, look at a painting, etc. we are engaged in sign-based representational behaviour. Representation has endowed the human species with the ability to cope effectively with the crucial aspects of existence – knowing, behaving purposefully, planning, socializing, and communicating. However, since representational activities vary from culture to culture, the signs people use on a daily basis constitute a mediating template in the worldview they come to have.

Types of Signs

There are six major types of signs that semiotics has catalogued and investigated, as we shall see in the remainder of this book.

Here it is useful simply to introduce them and characterize them generically. The first type of sign is the *symptom*. The bodies of all animals produce symptoms as warning signs, but what they indicate will depend on the species. As the biologist Jakob von Uexküll (1909) argued, the symptom is a reflex of anatomical structure. Animals with widely divergent anatomies will manifest virtually no symptomatology in common. It is interesting to note, by the way, that the term *symptom* is often extended metaphorically to refer to intellectual, emotional, and social phenomena that result from causes that are perceived to be analogous to physical processes: 'Their behaviour is a *symptom* of our times'; 'Their dislike of each other is a *symptom* of circumstances'; etc.

A second type of sign is the *signal*. All animals are endowed with the capacity to use and respond to species-specific signals for survival. Birds, for instance, are born prepared to produce a particular type of coo, and no amount of exposure to the songs of other species, or the absence of their own, has any effect on their cooing. A bird reared in isolation, in fact, will sing a very simple outline of the sort of song that would develop naturally in that bird born in the wild. This does not mean, however, that animal signalling is not subject to environmental or adaptational factors. Many bird species have also developed regional cooing 'dialects' by apparently imitating each other. Most signals are emitted automatically in response to specific types of stimuli and affective states. And because manifestations of animal signalling are truly remarkable, it is little wonder that they often trick people into seeing much more in them than is actually there. A well-known example of how easily people are duped by animal signalling is the case of *Clever Hans*, as will be discussed below.

A large portion of bodily communication among humans also unfolds largely in the form of unwitting signals. It has been shown, for example, that men are sexually attracted to women with large pupils, which signal unconsciously a strong and sexually tinged interest as well as making females look younger. This would explain the fashion vogue in central Europe during the 1920s and 1930s of women using a crystalline alkaloid eye-drop liquid derived from belladonna ('beautiful woman' in Italian). The women of the day used this drug because they believed – and correctly so, it would appear – that it would enhance facial appearance and sexual attractiveness by dilating the pupils.

But humans are capable as well of deploying witting signals for some intentional purpose – e.g., nodding, winking, glancing, looking, nudging, kicking, head tilting. As the psychologist Karl Bühler (1934: 28) aptly observed, such signals act like regulators, eliciting or inhibiting some action or reaction. Signalling systems can also be created for conventional social purposes. The list of such systems is extensive, and includes railway signals, smoke signals, semaphores, telegraph signals, Morse code signals, warning lights, flares, beacons, balefires, red flags, warning lights, traffic lights, alarms, distress signals, danger signals, whistles, sirens, bleepers, buzzers, knocking, gongs, bells, and drums.

The next three types of signs are taken from Peirce's classification of signs as *icons*, *indexes*, and *symbols*. An *icon* is a sign that is made to resemble, simulate, or reproduce its referent in some way. Photographs may be iconic signs because they can be seen to reproduce their referents in a visual way. Onomatopoeic words are also iconic signs because they simulate their referents in an acoustic way. Commercially produced perfumes that are suggestive of certain natural scents are likewise iconic, because they simulate the scents in an artificial way. The list could go on and on. The manifestations of iconicity can be seen across species, suggesting that the ability to manufacture concrete simulative representations of the world, consciously or unconsciously, is a basic semiosic capacity in most (if not all) life forms.

An *index* is a sign that refers to something or someone in terms of its existence or location in time or space, or in relation to something or someone else. Smoke is an index of fire pointing out where the fire is; a cough is an index of a cold; and so on. These signs do not resemble their referents, like icons; they indicate or show where they are. The most typical manifestation of indexicality is the pointing *index* finger, which humans the world over use instinctively to point out and locate things, people, and events in the world. Many words, too, manifest an implicit form of indexicality: e.g., *here, there, up,* and *down* refer to the relative location of things when we are speaking about them.

A *symbol* is a sign that stands for its referent in an arbitrary, conventional way. Most semioticians agree that symbolicity is what sets human representation apart from that of all other species, allowing the human species to reflect upon the world separately from stimulus-response situations. Words in general are symbolic signs. But any signifier – object, sound, figure, etc. – can be symbolic. A cross figure can stand for the concept 'Christianity'; a V-sign made with the index and middle fingers can stand symbolically for the concept 'victory'; *white* is a colour that can be symbolic of 'cleanliness,' 'purity,' or 'innocence,' but *dark* of 'uncleanness,' 'impurity,' or 'corruption'; and the list could go on and on. These symbols are all established by social convention.

The sixth, and final, type of sign to be discussed in this book is the *name.* This is an identifier sign assigned to the member of a species in various ways, as we shall see subsequently, that sets the specific member off from the others. A human name is a sign that identifies the person in terms of such variables as ethnicity and gender. Added names (surnames, nicknames, etc.) further refine the 'identity referent' of the name.

Nonverbal Communication

One of the main targets of a biological study of semiosis is *nonverbal communication.* Indeed, it is the 'default mode' of communication. Only the members of the species Homo sapiens are capable of communicating, simultaneously or in turn, by both nonverbal and verbal means. The expression 'by verbal means' is equivalent to some such expression as 'by means of speech,' or 'by means of script,' or 'by means of a sign language' (e.g., for use in a deaf group), that are, each, manifestations of any prerequisite natural language with which human beings are singularly endowed. However, not all humans are literate or can even speak: infants normally do develop a capacity for speaking, but only gradually; some adults never acquire speech; and others lose speech as a result of some trauma (e.g., a stroke) or in consequence of aging. Such conditions notwithstanding, humans lacking a capacity to verbalize – speak, write, or sign – can, as a rule, continue to communicate nonverbally.

The word *language* is sometimes used in common parlance in an inappropriate way to designate a certain nonverbal communicative device. Such may be confusing in this context where, if at all, 'language' should be used only in a technical sense, in reference to humans. Metaphorical uses such as 'body language,' 'the language of flowers,' 'the language of bees,' 'ape language,' or the like, are to be avoided.

Nonverbal communication takes place within an organism or between two or more organisms. Within an organism, participators in communicative acts may involve – as message sources or destinations or both – on rising integration levels, cellular organelles, cells, tissues, organs, and organ systems. In addition, basic features of the whole biological organization, conducted nonverbally in the *milieu intérieur,* include protein synthesis, metabolism, hormone activity, transmission of nervous impulses, and so forth. Communication on this level is usually studied (among other sciences) by subdomains of *biosemiotics* labelled *protosemiotics, microsemiotics, cytosemiotics,* or, comprehensively, *endosemiotics.*

Internal communication takes place by means of chemical, thermal, mechanical, and electrical sign operations, or semiosis, consisting of unimaginably busy trafficking. Take, as an example, a single human body, which consists of some 25 trillion cells, or about 2000 times the number of living earthlings, and consider further that these cells have direct or indirect connections with one another through messages delivered by signs in diverse modalities. The sheer density of such transactions is staggering. Only a minuscule fraction is known to us, let alone understood. Interior messages include information about the significance of one somatic scheme for all of the others, for each over-all control grid (such as the immune system), and for the entire integrative regulatory circuitry, especially the brain.

The earliest forms of interorganismic communication in our biosphere are found in prokaryotes – that is, mostly one-celled creatures lacking a nucleus. These are commonly called *bacteria.* In the last two decades, bacterial associations have come to be viewed as being of three sorts: localized teams; a single global superorganism; and those in interactions with eukaryotes (which are familiar life forms composed of cells having a membrane-bounded nucleus, notably animals and plants, but also several others). Localized teams of great complexity exist everywhere on earth: there are intestinal bacteria, dental-plaque bacteria, bacterial mats, and others. There is of course a very large bacterial population in both soils and the sludge at the bottom of bodies of waters. Such teams busily draw upon information fitting particular sets of circumstances, especially as regards the exchange of genetic information. A local bacterial team can adopt sophisticated communicative survival strategies, that is, it can function for a certain period of time as a single multicellular organism.

Bacteria have the potential to act in concert, that is, in the manner of a boundless planetary aggregation, as a sort of vast biological communications network – an Internet, so to speak. This ensemble has been characterized as a *superorganism*, possessing more basic information than the brain of any mammal, and whose myriad parts are capable of shifting and sharing information to accommodate to any and all circumstances.

The bacterial superorganism created environmental conditions conducive to the evolution of an entirely different life form: the eukaryotes. Bacteria exploited the eukaryotes as habitats as well as using them for vehicles to advance their own further dispersal. Indeed, eukaryotes evolved in consequence of a succession of intimate intracellular associations among prokaryotes. Biologists call such associations *symbioses*, but as these crucially entail diverse nonverbal communicative processes, they might more generally be characterized as forms of biological semioses. Biosemioses between bacterial entities started more than a thousand million years ago and are thus at the root of all communication.

Both in form and in the variety of their communicative transactions, animals are the most diverse of living creatures. Estimates of the number of animal species range from about three million up to more than thirty million. Since the behaviour of every species differs from that of every other – most of which are in any case scarcely fathomed – it will be evident that only a few general observations can be made here.

Animals communicate through different channels or combinations of media. Any form of energy propagation can, in fact, be exploited for purposes of message transmission. The convoluted ramifications of these can only be hinted at here. Take acoustic events as one set of illustrations. Since sound emission and sound reception are so ubiquitous in human communication, it may come as something of a surprise how rare sound is in the wider scheme of biological existence. In fact, the great majority of animals are both deaf and dumb. True hearing and functional sound production is prevalent – although by no means universal – only among the two most advanced phyla: the invertebrate Arthropods and the vertebrate Chordates (to which we also belong). Among the former, the insects far outnumber the rest of the animal kingdom. Sound is most widespread in the Orthoptera among these, including grasshoppers, especially the katydids, mantises, and cockroaches, and the cicadas of the order of Homoptera. Possessing the most complex of arthropodan sound-producing mechanisms, they also have well-developed hearing organs on the forepart of their abdomen. The Coleoptera, or beetles, contain quite a number of noisy forms. By contrast, sound use is rather rare among the Arachnids, which include ticks, mites, scorpions, and spiders.

As we move on to the vertebrates, it becomes useful to distinguish not only nonverbal from verbal but also nonvocal from vocal communication, and to introduce yet further discriminations with the advent of tools. The vocal mechanism that works by means of a current of air passing over the vocal cords, setting them into vibration, seems to be confined to ourselves and, with distinctions, to our nearest relatives, the other mammals, the birds (endowed with a syrinx), the reptiles, and the amphibians; although some fish do use wind instruments as well, they do so without the reed constituted by our vocal cords. So far as we know, no true vocal performances are found outside the land vertebrates or their marine descendants (such as whales).

Humans communicate via many channels, only one of which is

the acoustic. Acoustic communication among us may be both verbal and vocal, such as of course very commonly as we speak. But so-called alternative sign languages developed by emitters/receivers to be employed on special occasions or during times when speech is not permitted or is rendered difficult by special circumstances are, though generally verbal, not vocal. In this category are included North and South American Indian sign languages, Australian aboriginal sign languages, monastic communication systems actualized under a religious ban of silence, and certain occupational or performance sign languages, as in pantomime theatre or some varieties of ballet. Unvoiced signing may also be freely chosen in preference to speech when secrecy is wanted – for instance, when a baseball catcher prefers to keep the batter ignorant of the next type of pitch to be made; or if a criminal attempts to keep certain messages from witnesses. More complex sign languages used for secrecy are those employed by religious cults or secret societies, where ritual codes are meant to manipulate problematic social relationships between 'insiders' vs 'outsiders.'

Acoustic communication in humans may, moreover, be somatic or artefactual. This is well illustrated by contrasting humming or so-called 'whistle talk,' produced by the body alone, with 'drum signalling,' which requires some sort of percussion instrument (or at least a tree trunk). Sometimes nonverbal acoustic messages – with or without speech – are conveyed at a remove, from behind masks, through inanimate figures, such as puppets or marionettes, or through other performing objects. Again, acoustic somatic communication might be vocal, like a fearsome shriek, or nonvocal, like snapping one's fingers to summon a waiter. Furthermore, in humans, nonverbal communication in the acoustic mode, in all known communities, has been artfully elaborated into a large variety of musical realizations. These might be accompanied by a verbal text (as in a song), or crooned without lyrics, or produced by all sorts of musical instruments, or embedded in an enormously complex, multidimensional work of art, like an opera. Thus, while the overture to Mozart's *Don Giovanni* is a pure sonata-allegro, the enchanting Act I duet between the Don and Zerlina, 'Là ci darem la mano,' immediately following a *secco* (i.e., purely verbal) recitative, gives way to a melody solo then voices intertwining, climaxing in a gesture of physical touching and, dancelike (i.e., 6/8 meter) skipping off-stage arm in arm ('Andiam, andiam mio bene'). An opera being the supremely syncretic art form, Mozart's musical code, with Lorenzo da Ponte's libretto, is in this scene supported by a host of additional nonverbal artistic codes, such as mime, scenery, setting, costuming, and lighting, among others (as, elsewhere in the same opera, dancing, the culinary art, and even statuary).

Perhaps somewhat less complicated but comparably fused artistic structures include sound films. These usually partake of at least four codes: one visual and three auditory, including speech, music, and sound effects. Circus acrobatic performances, which are realized through at least five codes – the performer's dynamic behaviour, his or her social behaviour, the costumes and other accessories, the verbal accompaniment, and the musical accompaniment – furnish still another blended artistic achievement. The dazzling complexity of the messages generated by theatre events (Hamlet's '... suit the action to the word, the word to the action' providing but a modest start) can only be hinted at here.

Another interesting sort of nonverbal communication takes place during conducting, which can be defined as involving the elicitation of maximum of acoustical results from an orchestra with the most appropriate minimum choreographic gestures. In a public setting, the conductor connects not just with the members of the orchestra but also with the audience attending the concert. The gestures shaped by his entire upper-body equipment – including hands, arms, shoulders, head, and eyes – are decoded by the players and transformed into sound, which is then fed back to the audience. (Operatic conductors also often mouth lyrics.) As the eminent pianist Charles Rosen recently wrote: 'For all of us, music is bodily gesture as well as sound, and its primitive connection with dance is never entirely distilled away.'

The functional advantages or disadvantages of the different channels of communication have never been fully analysed, but certain statements can be made about acoustic communication in these respects which, other things being equal, apply to animals including man. A clear disadvantage, in contrast for instance to molecular traces such as pheromones (chemical messengers), which tend to persist over time, is the short-lived character of sound. To counteract this transience, humans eventually had recourse to writing and, more recently, introduced all sorts of sound-recording devices. This apparent defect may be outweighed by several advantages sound has over other media. For one thing, sound is independent of light and therefore can be used day or night. For another, it fills the entire space around the source. Accordingly, it does not require a straight line of connection with the destination. Moreover, it involves a minuscule expenditure of energy. In most animals, the body alone produces sound – ordinarily, no tool is requisite. In the case of humans, it can also be modulated to vary from intimate whisper to long-distance shouting.

In summarizing what is known of the acoustic behaviour of vertebrates, we can only scratch the surface here. Among fish, as in the insects, sound production seems to occur but sporadically. Almost all instances are in the Teleosts, and their methods are of three distinct kinds: by stridulation of one hard part against another (grinding their teeth, for instance); by expulsion of gas (a sort of breathing sound); or by vibrating their gas bladder. Some fish hiss like a cat, some growl, some grunt like a pig; others croak, snore, or croon; some bellow, purr, buzz, or whistle; one even vibrates like a drum. And of course fish can hear (although their auditory powers vary considerably).

Most amphibians cannot hear and seldom produce any sound other than a weak squeak, but frogs and toads are quite noisy in highly diverse ways. Reptiles can in general hear better; yet few produce sounds (though crocodiles roar and grunt).

Birds signify by sounds, given and received, but, more comprehensively, by so-called displays – stereotyped motor patterns involved in communication – which also include visual movements and posturing. Birds produce a huge variety of vocalizations, ranging from short, monosyllabic calls, to long, complicated sequences, their songs. Some birds can more or less faithfully reproduce, that is to say, 'parrot,' noises of their environment, imitating those of other species, notably even speech sounds. The communication systems of birds, which have been well studied for many centuries, are so heterogeneous that they cannot be dealt with here adequately. The same must be said of their multifarious, often dazzling, visible displays – stereotyped motor patterns – including their sometimes spectacular plumage (e.g., in peacocks or birds of paradise) and their constructs (as in bowerbirds).

Mammals have elaborate auditory organs and rely on the sense of hearing more than do members of any other group, but they also, like many birds, communicate, if sporadically, by nonvocal methods as well. A familiar example of this is the drumming behaviour in the gorilla, produced by clenched fists beating on the chest. Echolocation refers to the phenomenon where the emitter and receiver of a train of sounds is the same individual; this is found in bats as well as marine mammals, such as certain species of whales and dolphins. (The capability of blind people to navigate by echolocation has not been proved.) Some vertebrates, like rats, mice, gerbils, and hamsters, communicate in a range inaudible to normal human hearing, by ultrasonic calls. (Analogously, the most effective colour for the social bees seems to be ultraviolet, outside the spectrum of unaided human vision.)

All carnivores (cats, dogs, hyenas, etc.) as well as all primates more or less vigorously vocalize, including man's closest relatives, the apes. But the characteristic performances of these creatures are both so rich and varied – from the relatively silent orangutans to the remarkably diverse 'singing' gibbons – that describing them would demand a book-length treatment. Instead of attempting to even sketch these here, it's worth emphasizing that apes do not communicate verbally in the wild and that, furthermore, even the most strenuous undertakings to inculcate any manifestation of any natural language in captive apes – contrary to insistent claims made in the media – have uniformly failed.

Attempts to teach language-like skills to apes or to any other animals (such as captive marine mammals or pet birds) have been extensively criticized on the grounds that the Clever Hans effect, or fallacy, might have been at work (as mentioned above). Since this phenomenon has profound implications for (among other possible dyads) man–animal communications of all sorts, some account seems in order here. In brief, a stallion named Hans, in Berlin at the turn of the century, was reputed to be able to do arithmetic and perform comparably impressive verbal feats, responding nonverbally to spoken or written questions put to him by tapping out the correct answers with his foot. Ingenious tests eventually proved that the horse was in fact reacting to nonverbal cues unwittingly given by the questioner. Ever since that demonstration of how unintended cueing can affect an experiment on animal behaviour, alert and responsible scientists have tried to exclude the sometimes highly subtle perseverance of the effect.

It later turned out that there are two variants of the Clever Hans fallacy: those based on self-deception, indulged in by Hans's owner/trainer and other interrogators; and those performances – with 'wonder horses,' 'talking dogs,' and 'learned' pigs or geese – based on deliberate trickery, performed by stage magicians and common con 'artists' (over many centuries). Deceptive nonverbal signalling pervades the world of animals and men. In animals, basic shapes of unwitting deception are known as mimicry.

This is usually taken to include the emulation of dangerous models by innocuous mimics in terms of visible or auditory signals, or distasteful scents, in order to fool predators. In humans, deceptive communications in daily life have been studied by psychologists, and, on the stage, by professional magicians. Various body parts may be mendaciously entailed, singly or in combination: gaze, pupil dilation, tears, winks, facial expression, smile or frown, gesture, posture, voice, etc.

A consideration of mainly acoustic events thus far should by no means be taken for neglect of other channels in which nonverbal messages can be encoded, among them chemical, optical, tactile, electric, and thermal. The chemical channel antedates all the others in evolution and is omnipresent in all organisms. Bacterial communication is exclusively chemical.

Plants interact with other plants via the chemical channel, and with animals (especially insects, but humans as well), in addition to the usual contact channels, by optical means. While the intricacies of plant communication (technically known as phytosemiosis) can not be further explored here, mention should at least be made of two related fields of interest: the pleasant minor semiotic artifice of floral arrangements; and the vast domain of gardens as major nonverbal semiosic constructs. Formal gardens, landscape gardens, vegetable gardens, water gardens, coral gardens, and Zen gardens are all remarkable nonverbal contrivances, which are variously cultivated from Malinowski's Trobriands to traditional Japanese kare sansui (dry garden), to Islamic lands, China, and, notably so, in France and Britain.

Smell (olfaction, odour, scent, aroma) is used for purposes of communication crucially, say, by sharks and hedgehogs, social insects such as bees, termites, and ants, and such social mammals as wolves and lions. It is less important in birds and primates, which rely largely on sight. In modern societies, smell has been roundly commercialized in the olfactory management of food and toiletry commodities, concerned with repulsive body odour and the effects of tobacco products. Perfumes are often associated with love and sexual potency.

The body by itself can be a prime tool for communication, verbal as well as nonverbal. Thus, in animals, it is well known that dogs and cats display their bodies in acts of submission and intimidation, as famously pictured in Charles Darwin's (1872) book on *The Expression of the Emotions in Man and Animals*. There are many striking illustrations in Desmond Morris's (1969) field guide *The Human Zoo*, and in the photos assembled by Weldon Kees (Ruesch and Kees 1956) of how the human frame is brought habitually into play. Professional wrestling is popular entertainment masquerading as a sport that features two or a group of writhing bodies, groaning and grunting, pretending in a quasi-morality play of good vs evil to vie for victory; the players obviously interact with one another, but, more subtlety, communicate with a live audience. Such performances differ from legitimate bouts involving boxing or collegiate wrestling, or sports like tennis matches, and group events, such as soccer or cricket, in that the outcome of the contest is hardly in suspense.

Dance is one sophisticated art form that can express human thought and feeling through the instrumentality of the body in many genres and in many cultures. One of these is Western ballet, which intermingles sequences of hand and limb gestural exchanges with flowing body movements and a host of other non-verbal protocols that echo one another, like music, costumes, lighting, masks, scenery, wigs, etc. Dance and music usually accompany pantomime or dumb shows. Silent clowns or mimes supplement their body movements by suitable make-up and costuming.

Facial expressions – pouting, the curled lip, a raised eyebrow, crying, flaring nostrils – constitute a powerful, universal communication system, solo or in concert. Eye work, including gaze and mutual gaze, can be particularly powerful in understanding a range of quotidian vertebrate as well as human social behaviour. Although the pupil response has been observed since antiquity, in the last couple of decades it has matured into a broad area of research called pupillometry. Among circus animal trainers it has long been an unarticulated rule to carefully watch the pupil movements of their charges, for instance tigers, to ascertain their mood alteration. Bears, on the contrary, are reported to be 'unpredictable,' hence dangerous, precisely because they lack the pupil display as well as owing to their inelastic muzzle, which thus cannot 'telegraph' an imminent attack. In interpersonal relationships between human couples a dilation in pupil size acts in effect as an unwitting message transmitted to the other person (or an object) of an intense, often sexually toned, interest.

Many voluminous dictionaries, glossaries, manuals, and source books exist to explicate and illustrate the design and meaning of brands, emblems, insignia, signals, symbols, and other signs (in the literal, tangible sense), including speech-fixing signs such as script and punctuation, numerical signs, phonetic symbols, signatures, trademarks, logos, watermarks, heraldic devices, astrological signs, signs of alchemy, cabalistic and magical signs, talismans, technical and scientific signs (as in chemistry), pictograms, and other such imagery, many of them used extensively in advertising. Regulatory signs (*No Smoking*), direction signs deployed at airports (*Passport Control, Men, Women*) or in hospitals (*Pediatrics*), international road signs (*No Passing*) are commonly supplemented by icons under the pressure of the need for communication across language barriers, certain physical impairments, or comparable handicaps.

The labyrinthine ramifications of optical communication in the world of animals and for humanity are boundless and need to be dealt with separately. Such sciences as astronomy and the visual arts have, since prehistoric times, naturally and mainly unfolded in the optical channel. Alterations of the human body and its physical appearance, from non-permanent, such as body painting or theatrical make-up or routine hair service, to quasi-permanent metamorphoses, by dint of procedures such as body sculpture, e.g., the past Chinese 'lotus foot' or Western 'tight-lacing' customs; infibulation, cicatrization, or tattooing; and, more generally, plastic surgery, all convey messages – frequently, as reconstruction, cosmetic in intent, in female breast size – by nonverbal means. The art of mummy painting in Roman Egypt was intended to furnish surrogates for the head by which to facilitate silent communication of a deceased individual during his or her passage to the afterlife.

An intriguing variety of nonverbal human communicative-behaviour-at-a-remove features a bizarre form of barter known since Herodotus, modern instances of which are still reported, and labelled by ethnographers 'silent trade.' None of the common direct channels are usually involved, only the abstract idea of exchange. What happens is something like this: one party to a commercial transaction leaves goods at a prearranged place, then withdraws to a hidden vantage point to watch unobserved – or more likely not. The other party then appears and inspects the commodity left behind. If satisfied by the find, it leaves a comparable amount of some other articles of trade.

The study of spatial and temporal bodily arrangements (sometimes called *proxemics*) in personal rapport, the proper dimensions of a cage in the zoo or of a prison cell, the layout of offices, classrooms, hospital wards, exhibitions in museums and galleries, and myriad other architectural designs all involve the axiology of volume and duration. A map is a graphic representation of a milieu, containing both pictorial or iconic and non-pictorial or symbolic elements, ranging from a few simple configurations to highly complex blueprints or other diagrams and mathematical equations. All maps are also indexical. They range from the local, such as the well-known multicoloured representation of the London underground, to the intergalactic metal plaque on the Pioneer 10 spacecraft speeding its way out of our solar system. All organisms communicate by use of models (*Umwelts*, or self-worlds, each according to its species-specific sense organs), from the simplest representations of manoeuvres of approach and withdrawal to the most sophisticated cosmic theories of Newton and Einstein. It would be well to recall that Einstein originally constructed his model of the universe out of nonverbal signs, 'of visual and some of muscular type.' As he wrote to a colleague in 1945: 'The words or the language, as they are written or spoken, do not seem to play any role in my mechanism of thought. The psychical entities which seem to serve as elements in thought are certain signs and more or less clear images which can be "voluntarily" reproduced and combined.' Later, 'only in a secondary stage,' after long and hard labour to transmute his nonverbal construct into 'conventional words and other signs,' was he able to communicate it to others.

2

The Study of Signs

Consider what these ten little dramas have in common:

- A radiologist spots a silhouette on a chest X-ray photograph of a patient and diagnoses lung cancer.

- A meteorologist notes a rise in barometric pressure and delivers the next day's forecast taking that change into account.

- An anthropologist observes a complex of ceremonial exchanges practised among members of a tribe; she draws analytical insights into the polity, economy, and social organization of the people she is studying.

- A French-language teacher holds up a picture of a horse. His American pupil says, 'Horse.' The teacher shakes his head and pronounces, 'Cheval.'

- A historian takes a look at the handwriting of a former president and therefrom gains insight into her subject's personality.

- A Kremlin watcher, in the former Soviet Union, observes the proximity of a member of the politburo to the party secretary on May Day and surmises the member's current status.

- A compromising fingerprint is introduced as evidence in a trial; the defendant is convicted on that evidence.

- A hunter notices in the snow sets of rectangular tracks of pointed hoofs with an impression of dew claws; the forefoot track is 15 cm long and 13 cm broad, and the corresponding measurements for the hind-foot track are 15 cm and 11 cm. There are spherical droppings on the trail 20–30 mm long and 15–20 mm broad. The hunter surmises, with a high degree of probability, that a fully grown bull elk is trotting ahead of him.

- A man finds himself being stared at by a dog, growling, barking, head held high and neck arched, lips contracted vertically and teeth bared, ears erect and turned forward. The man concludes he is in danger of imminent attack and takes evasive action.

- A peacock displays to a susceptible peahen; she circles rapidly and squats. Coition ensues.

Those of us who practise *semiotics* tend to treat these happenings the same way despite their manifest substantive differences of setting, cast of human or speechless characters, and many other variables. What entitles us to do so is an abstractive operation which resolves each episode to an instance of *semiosis,* or sign action. In this view, semiotics is not about the 'real' world at all, but about complementary or alternative actual models of it and – as Leibniz thought – about an infinite number of anthropologically conceivable possible worlds. Thus semiotics never reveals what the world is, but circumscribes what we can know about it; in other words, what a semiotic model depicts is not 'reality' as such, but nature as unveiled by our method of questioning. It is the interplay between 'the book of nature' and its human decipherer that is at issue. The distinction may be pictured by the simile of a fisherman casting his net; the size of the fish he can catch is limited by the morphology of the net, but this fact does not provide tutorage in ichthyology. A concept of 'modelling systems' has been central to the semiotics of the so-called Moscow-Tartu school since the 1960s, but, having been derived from a representation of language in structural linguistics, it has focused on culture to the exclusion of the rest of nature. In the age-old philosophical quest for reality, two alternative points of departure have been suggested: that the structure of being is reflected in semiotic structures, which thus constitute models, or maps, of reality; or that the reverse is the case, namely, that semiotic structures are independent variables so that reality becomes the dependent variable. Although both views are beset by many difficulties, a version of the second, proposed by the remarkably seminal Estonian biologist Jakob von Uexküll (1864–1944), under the watchword *Umwelt-Forschung* – approximately translated as 're-search in subjective universes' – has proved to be in best conformity with modern semiotics (as well as with ethology). The same attitude was expressed by Niels Bohr when he answered an objection that reality is more fundamental than the language it underlies; Bohr replied: 'We are suspended in language in such a way that we cannot say what is up and what is down' (French and Kennedy 1985: 302). Signs have acquired their effectiveness through evolutionary adaptation to the vagaries of the sign wielder's *Umwelt*. When the *Umwelt* changes, these signs can become obstacles, and the signer, extinct.

A Biological Approach to the Study of Signs

According to the incomparable philosopher and polymath Charles Sanders Peirce (1839–1914), who has justly been called 'the most original and the most versatile intellect that the Americas have so far produced' (Fisch 1980: 1) and who uniquely reinvigorated semiotics, the antique doctrine of signs, semiosis involves an irreducibly triadic relation among a sign, its object, and its interpretant. This trio of terms and their next of kin have far-resounding philosophical overtones. Before rehearsing some of these, let me dwell on a common definition of semiotics and pause to consider its components and a few of its consequences. The subject matter of semiotics, it is often credited, is the exchange of any messages whatsoever – in a word, *communication.* To this must at once be added that semiotics is also focally concerned with the study of *signification.* Semiotics is therefore classifiable as that pivotal branch of an integrated science of communication to which its character as a methodical inquiry into the nature and constitution of codes provides an indispensable counterpoint.

A message is a sign or a string of signs transmitted from a sign producer, or source, to a sign receiver, or destination. Any source or any destination is a living entity or the product of a living entity, such as a computer, a robot, automata in general, or a postulated supernatural being, as when a boy (source), on bent knees (non-verbal message), beseeches his deity (destination), 'I pray the Lord my soul to take' (verbal message). It is important to realize that only living things and their inanimate extensions undergo semiosis, which thereby becomes uplifted as a necessary, if not sufficient, criterial attribute of life. By 'living things' are meant not just the organisms belonging to one of the five kingdoms, consisting of the Monera, Protoctista, Animalia, Plantae, and Fungi, but also their hierarchically developed choate component parts, beginning with a cell, the minimal semiosic unit, estimated to correspond to about fifty genes, or about one thousand billion (10^{12}) intricately organized atoms. (Viruses are omitted because they are neither cells nor aggregations of cells.) Our bodies are assemblages of cells, about one hundred thousand billion (10^{14}) of them, harmoniously attuned to one another by an incessant flux of vital messages. The origin of nucleated cells is a dimly apprehended story of the symbiotic and semiosic collaboration among single cells – populations of blue algae and bacteria without apparent internal components; they evolved less than one billion years after the formation of Earth (and ample traces of them were harvested in Greenland). Simple cells, it is thought, fused to form the complex confederations of cells composing each living being. They, in turn, are integrated into organs, organs into organisms, forming social systems of ever-increasing complexity. Thus, physics, biology, psychology, and sociology each embodies its own peculiar level of semiosis. The genetic code governs the exchange of messages on the cellular level; hormones and neurotransmitters mediate among organs and between one another (the immune defence system and the central nervous system are intimately inter-wreathed by a dense flow of two-way message traffic); and a variety of non-verbal and verbal messages conjoin organisms into a network of relations with each other as well as with the rest of their environment. As François Jacob picturesquely described (1974: 320) the progression, 'from family organization to modern state, from ethnic group to coalition of nations, a whole series of integrations is based on a variety of cultural, moral, social, political, economic, military and religious codes. The history of mankind is more or less the history of these integrons and the way they form and change.' Semiosis on a superior level in the hierarchy of integrons is reducible to that on a lower level, namely, ultimately to physics (Popper and Eccles 1977).

The semiosic comportment of even the major organismic groupings, with differing lifestyles, has been unevenly studied. In the web of nature, plants are, above all, producers; an examination of their communicative behaviour, under the banner of 'phytosemiotics,' began only in 1981, when the German semiotician Martin Krampen published an insightful programmatic article under that title. The polar opposites of plants are the fungi, nature's decomposers; our knowledge of their peculiar brand of semiosis is even more rudimentary. Primary interest has hitherto focused on animals (zoosemiotics), the ingesters, which mediate between the other two and, according to what they consume, may be categorized either as herbivores or predators; their nutritional mode may also mark the character of their respective reliance on sign use.

Note the message traffic in four out of the five kingdoms is exclusively non-verbal; verbal messages have been found only in animals and there surge solely in one extant subspecies, *Homo sapiens sapiens*. The most distinctive trait of humans is that only they, throughout terrestrial life, have two separate, although, of course, thoroughly commingled, repertoires of signs at their disposal: the non-verbal – demonstrably derived from their mammalian (especially primate) ancestry – and a uniquely human verbal overlay. The latter constitutes the subject matter of the most advanced and highly formalized branch of semiotics, *general linguistics*, the study of verbal commerce and its subjacent grammatical foundation.

The definition advanced here presupposes a message producer, or source, and a message receiver, or destination. In the examples above, extant or formerly alive sources and destinations figure in such roles as those of patient and physician; ethnographic field-worker and informants; teacher and pupil; historian and late public figure; remote foreign official and political scientist; elk and hunter; dog and potential victim; peacock and peahen. The barometer read by the weather forecaster is a human-made instrument of observation, one of a class of sense-enhancing devices, such as a bubble chamber, constructed to render ineffable messages effable; thus no physicist can really 'see' subatomic particles, not even aided by the most powerful electron microscope (or accelerator-detector complex), but only (in the simple case) the tiny bubbles of hydrogen produced by them – the vaporous beads in the tank 'stand for,' that is, model, their interactions. As for the dermatoglyph presented to the court, this functions here as a probatively synecdochic message-by-contiguity about the guilt of a presumed criminal.

In any given transaction, a source is necessarily coupled by means of a channel to a destination; the variety of such passageways is constrained by the specific sensorium of each. This state of affairs was neatly summed up by George Dalgarno (the Scottish author of *Ars signorum*, a fascinating semiotic treatise from the mid-seventeenth century): 'It is true,' he wrote in 1680, 'that all the Senses are Intelligencers to the Soul less or more; for tho they have their distinct limits, and proper Objects assigned them by nature; yet she is able to use their service even in the most abstracted Notions, and Arbitrary institution.' Dalgarno adds that 'nature seems to have fitted two, Hearing and Seeing, more particularly for her service,' but this is a superficial view. By far the most hoary messages are molecular, and the chemical channel is the most prevalent. Three of the hierarchical levels of basic endosemiotic control are regulated, respectively, by the genetic code, by humoral as well as cell-mediated immune reactions, and (since the appearance of the sponges) by the large number of peptides present in the central nervous system, functioning as neurotransmitters. The olfactory and gustatory senses are likewise semiochemical. Even in vision, the impact of photons on the retina differentially affects the capacity of the pigment rhodopsin, which fills the rods to absorb light of different wavelengths, the condition for the univariance principle. Acoustic and tactile vibrations, and impulses delivered via the thermal senses, are, as well, finally transformed into electrochemical messages. Humans and many other animals are routinely linked by several channels simultaneously or in succession. Parallel processing of messages introduces a degree of redundancy, by virtue of which it becomes more likely that errors in reception will be minimized; however, it is also possible for collimated messages to contradict one another – this is how a rhetorical figure such as irony performs in spoken or written discourse, as does the back-arch display of a house cat in zoosemiotics.

Messages

It is unknown how most sources generate – or, to use a less overburdened term, formulate – a message. Human beings are capable of launching an enormous number of novel messages appropriate to an indefinite variety of contexts, but the electrochemical intricacies of their initial entrainment by that cramped globe of tissue known as the brain remain an enigma. Plainly, however, the message-as-formulated must undergo a transductive operation to be externalized into serial strings appropriate to the channel, or channels, selected to link up with the destination. This neurobiological transmutation from one form of energy to another is called *encoding*. When the destination detects and extracts the encoded messages from the channel, another transduction, followed by a series of still further transformations, must be effected before interpretation can occur; this pivotal reconversion is called *decoding*. Encoding and decoding imply a code, a set of unambiguous rules whereby messages are convertible from one representation to another; the code is what the two parties in the message exchange are supposed to have, in fact or by assumption, totally or in part, in common. Using Joseph Weizenbaum's famous computer program, aptly named *Eliza*, human interlocutors tend to project sympathy, interest, and intelligence upon Eliza, as they would upon a psychotherapist. In fact, Eliza 'knows' nothing. A similar fallacy about shared codes is the theme of Jerzy Kosinski's brilliant novelette *Being There* (and the faithful movie based on it), in which an illiterate, retarded gardener is ascribed supreme gnostic attributes because he – essentially a blank page – mimics, echoes, and reflects back the interactive codes of every one of his conversational partners, whatever their native speech community may be.

Receivers interpret messages as an amalgam of two separate but inextricably blended inputs: the physical triggering sign, or signal, itself, but as unavoidably shaped by *context*. The latter plays a cardinal role, yet the concept has eluded definition; too, it is generally unknown how destinations 'take into account' context. In semiotics the term is used both broadly and loosely to encompass preceding messages (anaphoric presuppositions), and probably succeeding messages (cataphoric implicatures), environmental and semantic noise, all filtered by short- and long-term memory, genetic and cultural.

The Sign

These six key factors – messages and code, source and destination, channel and context – separately and together make up the rich domain of semiotic researches. However, the pivotal notion remains the *sign*. This term has been defined in many different ways since its introduction in ancient Greece. In medical semiotics, for example, sign has been used in conjunction with, or, rather, in opposition to, *symptom* since at least Alcmaeon, Hippocrates, and especially Galen (A.D. c.130–c.200). Clinical practitioners usually distinguish between 'soft data,' or subjective signs, dubbed symptoms, meaning by this whatever the patient relates verbally about his/her feelings ('I have a pain in my chest') or exhibits non-verbally (groans while pointing to the chest); and 'hard data,' or objective signs, which clinicians actually call 'signs,' meaning whatever the physician observes with his/her eyes and ears (bloody sputum, wheezing) or with his/her instruments (shadow on an X-ray photograph). Many philosophers also use the term *sign*; however, not a few contrast it with *symbol* rather than with symptom. The neo-Kantian, twentieth-century philosopher Ernst Cassirer (1874–1945), for instance, claimed that these two notions belonged to different universes of discourse, and that 'a sign is a part of the physical world, a symbol is a part of the human world of meaning' (Cassirer 1944: 32). Minimalist approaches such as these are far too imprecise and superficial to be serviceable, as Peirce painstakingly demonstrated throughout his voluminous writings. For Peirce, *sign* was a generic concept, of which there are a very large number of species, multiplying from a trichotomous base of *icon*, index, and *symbol*, each defined according to that sign category's relation to its object in a particular context.

To clarify what a sign is, it is useful to begin with the medieval formula *aliquid stat pro aliquo*, broadened by Peirce, about 1897, to something which stands to somebody for something in some respect or capacity. To the classic notion of *substitution* featured in this famous phrase – Roman Jakobson called it *renvoi*, translatable as 'referral' – Peirce here added the criterion of *interpretation*. At this point, let us take a closer look at the object-sign-interpretant trichotomous cycle alluded to earlier, and also pause to consider Peirce's 'somebody,' the destination or other receiver of the message.

The initial distinction between object (O) and sign (S) raises profound questions about the anatomy of reality, indeed about its very existence, but there is nothing approaching a consensus about these riddles among physicists, let alone philosophers. One obvious implication of this postulated duality is that semiosis requires at least two actants: the observer and the observed. Our intuition of reality is a consequence of a mutual interaction between the two: Jakob von Uexküll's private world of elementary sensations (*Merkzeichen*, 'perceptual signs') coupled to their meaningful transforms into action impulses (*Wirkzeichen*, 'operation signs'); and the phenomenal world (*Umwelt*), that is, the subjective world each animal models out of its 'true' environment (*Natur*, 'reality'), which reveals itself solely through signs. The rules and laws to which those sign processes – namely, semiosis – are subject are the only actual laws of nature. 'As the activity of our mind is the only piece of nature known to us,' he argued in his great work, *Theoretical Biology*, 'its laws are the only ones that have the right to be called laws of Nature' (Uexküll 1973 [1928]: 40).

Any observer's version of his/her *Umwelt* will be one unique model of the world, which is a system of signs made up of genetic factors plus a cocktail of experiences, including future expectations. A complicating fact of life is that the bare act of observation entails a residual juncture that disturbs the system being observed. The essential ingredient, or nutriment, of mind may well be information, but to acquire information about anything requires, via a long and complex chain of steps, the transmission of signs from the object of interest to the observer's central nervous system. Its attainment, moreover, takes place in such a manner that this influential action reacts back upon the object being observed so as to perturb its condition. In brief, the brain, or mind, which is itself a system of signs, is linked to the putative world of objects, not simply by perceptual selection, but by such a far-off remove from physical inputs – sensible stimuli – that we can safely assert that the only cognizance any animal can possess, 'through a glass, darkly,' as it were, is that of signs. Whether there is a reality behind signs – perhaps what Heraclitus called *logos*, the repeatable structure that secures for any object its ideal unity and stability, and which the French topologist René Thom (1975) and I have independently rendered as 'form' – humanity can never be sure. As Heraclitus so eloquently put it, 'You could not discover the limits of soul, even if you travelled every road to do so; such is the depth of its form.' In sum, this reasoning entitles us to rewrite O as S_{O_n}, so that the initial twofold distinction is resolved to one between two sorts of signs.

What about the third correlate, Peirce's *interpretant* (I)? What did he mean by this much-discussed (and even more often misunderstood) concept? True, no single, canonical definition of it is to be found in his writings, but he does make it clear that every sign determines an interpretant 'which is itself a sign, [so that] we have a sign overlying sign.' He also points out that an interpretant can be either an equivalent sign or 'perhaps a more developed sign,' which is where novelty enters the system, enabling us to increase our understanding of the immediate object. To illustrate all this, ponder some interpretants of the English noun *horse*. They could be (partial) synonyms such as *colt, gee-gee, gelding, hinny, mare, pony, stallion, stud, thoroughbred* – to say nothing of heroin – and the like, or the interpretant could be a monolingual rewording, including standard dictionary definitions, such as the *OED*'s: 'A solid-hoofed perissodactyl quadruped ... having a flowing mane and tail, whose voice is a neigh.' Another of its interpretants is the scientific name *Equus Przewalski caballus*, as are all (roughly) equivalent translations into verbal signs in other languages, such as *cheval, Pfred, losad, hevonen*, and so forth. Historical tokens, such as Bucephalus, Morocco, Clever Hans, and all the Lipizzaners of the Spanish Riding School of Vienna belong here, as do such literary representations as Dean Swift's Houyhnhnms, Peter Shaffer's play *Equus*, Conan Doyle's saga *Silver Blaze*, Eco's creature Brunellus, and entire scientific treatises as different as Xenophon's disquisition *Treatise on Horsemanship*, Stefan von Maday's *Psychologie der Pferde und der Dressur*, and E.H. Gombrich's penetrating essay 'Meditations on a Hobby Horse.' Intersemiotic transmutations into nonverbal signs include innumerable and worldwide engravings and paintings of horses (notably from the Magdalenian caves), sculptures (from the Neolithic period onward, including those of the Chinese tradition since Lung-shan Scythian friezes, Greek centaurs, as well as modern filmic portrayals such as *National Velvet* and *The Black Stallion*. Finally, of course, any 'actual' horse I point to may become, by virtue of that gesture, which is an indexical sign, or an 'object of direct experience so far as it directs attention to an object by which its presence is caused,' an interpretant. There is no doubt that an intralingual synonym or paraphrase of, or extended discourse on, any sign will enrich comprehension of the object it represents, as will also its interlingual translations and intersemiotic transmutations. Each further interpretant tends to amplify intelligence and afford opportunity for a cascade of semantic innovation and therefore change. (Another, more technical, way of putting this is that any metalanguage explicating an object language is always richer than the latter.)

In brief, it follows from Peirce's way of looking at the sign that the second distinction, as much as the first, resolves itself into two sorts of signs, to wit, S and S_{I_n}. Once more, here are his words: a sign is anything 'which determines something else (its *interpretant*) to refer to an object to which itself refers (its *object*) in the same way, the sign becoming in turn a sign, and so on *ad infinitum.*'

Signs and 'Reality'

If objects are signs, in indefinite regression to a supposititious *logos*, and if interpretants are signs marching in progression toward the ultimate disintegration of mind, what is there left that is not a sign? What of the 'somebody' mentioned by Peirce – the observer or the interpreter of the train after train of sign actions? In a celebrated article he published in 1868, Peirce anticipated and answered this question, contending that 'the word or sign which humans use are the humans themselves,' which is to claim that the human and the external sign are identical, in the same sense in which the words *homo* and *man* are identical. 'Thus my language is the sum total of myself, for the man is the thought.' In short, the 'somebody' is also a sign or a text. What of the human being's faculty of procreation, shared with all other life forms? Peirce showed that even this capacity is inherent in signs, a parallel that has been elaborated by Thom (1973). Signs come into being only by development out of other signs.

The position adverted to in the foregoing paragraphs, according to which, at a certain point in the semiosic cycle, there are objects, included among them conscious observers or interpreters – such as people, porpoises, and perhaps Phobians – and there are, at another point in the cycle, interpretants, both being kinds of signs, is a familiar one in philosophical tradition. This position – one that surely follows from Peirce's wistful, throw-away remark about something he took to be a fact, 'that the entire universe ... is perfused with signs, if it is not composed exclusively of signs' – is known as idealism, and that of a particular hue, sometimes called 'conceptual idealism,' which maintains that our view of reality, namely, our *Umwelt*, entails an essential reference to mind (*Gemüt*) in its constitution. As Kant insisted – and, of course, both Peirce and Jakob von Uexküll had thoroughly assimilated Kantian principles – 'raw experience' is unattainable; experience, to be apprehended, must first be steeped in, strained through, and seasoned by a soup of signs. For this reason, this brand of idealism can be called 'semi-otic idealism,' in the apt designation put forward by the philoso-pher David Savan (1983). Furthermore, to paraphrase Savan, semiotic idealism comes in two flavours, strong or radical and mild or tolerant, between which he leans toward the latter, namely, 'the thesis that any properties, attributes, or characteristics of whatever exists depend upon the system of signs, representations, or inter-pretations through which they are signified.' Without necessarily committing oneself to this or that brand of idealism – only the real-ist positions are, I think, altogether devoid of interest – it is clear that what semiotics is finally all about is the role of mind in the cre-ation of the world or of physical constructs out of a vast and diverse crush of sense impressions.

In 1984 I was an auditor at an international state-of-the-art con-ference, co-sponsored by Indiana University and the National Endowment for the Humanities. The topic debated was whether semiotics is a field or a discipline – a question Umberto Eco had suggested in a speech delivered ten years earlier on the Indiana campus. Most speakers were specialists in one or more of the com-plex historical sciences the French call *les sciences humaines*. The designated formal discussant was the late illustrious and sceptical English social anthropologist Sir Edmund Leach, who had de-tected undue hubris in the presentations, pointing out to the speakers that 'others were there before you.' As to that, he was undoubtedly correct. Obsessive concern with signs dates from the appearance of the most dramatic of all steps in hominoid evolu-tion, the emergence of verbal signs and the changes in informa-tion storage and transmission that accompanied that transition. The same preoccupation with signs is evident throughout infant and child development. When my five-year-old daughter asked me, 'Daddy, just what does the Salivation Army do?' and when another, who was seven years old, wondered just how Dracula was killed by a 'steak' driven into his heart, I knew I was not being led into the tangled thickets of philanthropy or Transylvania, but into that *locus classicus* of signs in action, paronomasia.

To conclude this second chapter, a caveat is in order. To say that semiotics is a 'human' or 'historical' science may well perpetuate an illusion. According to at least one version of quantum theory, John Archibald Wheeler's highly imaginative rendition of the so-called Copenhagen interpretation, the past is theory, or yet another system of signs; it 'has no existence except in the records of the present.' At a semiotic level we make the past as well as the present and the future.

3

Six Species of Signs

In this chapter I will first look at the general features that characterize signs. Then I will delineate a typology of six basic 'species' of signs which reflects the types of signs most regularly identified and commonly employed by semioticians.

General Features of Signs

There are a number of general features of signs that require some discussion at length. These are well-known features that have been investigated from various angles over the decades.

1. The Sign Is Bifacial

In 1305, in his unfinished treatise *De vulgari eloquentiae* (1957: 18), Dante proffered this formulation of the concept of the (verbal) sign: 'hoc equidem signum ... sensuale quid est, in quantum sonus est: rationale vero, in quantum aliquid significare videtur ad placitum.' This restatement is in good conformity with practically every model of the intrinsic structure of the sign that, with one emphasis or another, has been put forward in accounts dealing with the foundations of the doctrine of signs, ranging from Stoic philosophy to contemporary thinking. This expression implies that the sign is constituted of two indispensable moieties, one *aistheton*, perceptible (or sensible), the other *noeton*, intelligible (or rational): the *signifier*, an appreciable impact on at least one of the interpreter's sense organs, and the content *signified*. (In medieval Latin, the corresponding pair of terms for the Stoic *sémainon*, 'signifier,' and *sémainomenon*, 'signified,' was *signans* and *signatum*, rendered by Saussure as *signifiant* and *signifié*, in German usually as *das Signifikat* and *der Signifikant*, by Morris as *sign vehicle* and *designatum*, by some Soviet scholars [Revzina 1972: 231] as 'thing' and 'concept,' etc.)

2. Zero Signs

In various systems of signs, notably in language, a sign vehicle can sometimes – when the contextual conditions are appropriate – signify by its very absence, occur, that is, in *zero* form. Linguists who employ the expression 'zero sign' (zero phoneme or allophone, zero morpheme or allomorph, and the like) must mean either 'zero signifier,' or, much more rarely, 'zero signified,' but never both; if taken literally, the notion of a 'zero sign' would be oxymoronic. (On the use of zero in linguistics, see Jakobson 1940, 1966; Frei 1950; Godel 1953; Haas 1957.) The role of zero sign vehicles in communication systems other than the verbal has never been properly analysed. Pohl (1968: 34–5), for instance, erroneously remarks that civilian clothing functions as a zero when worn in a context of uniforms; but this confounds the unmarked/marked opposition with the realized/zero opposition.

Zero sign vehicles also occur in animal communication systems. Thus Ardrey (1970: 75) claims that the African 'elephant's alarm call is silence,' and so, too, René-Guy Busnel that the temporal parameter between the message exchanged by two members of the species *Laniarius erythogaster*, that is, 'the rhythmic pattern of silences ... and not the acoustic part of the signal itself' carries the information (Sebeok 1968: 138). But a heuristically more promising inquiry is suggested by the quasi-prosodic phenomenon that, in several types of fireflies, pulse interval is a significant element in stimulating females, and that these intervals are distinct in different species, for example, in *Photinus consanguineus* and *macdermotii*; in the related *lineellus*, furthermore, the pulse number is variable, 'which further indicates the significance of pulse interval' (Lloyd 1966: 78). The existence of zero forms in various systems of communication does not, therefore, vitiate the classic bipartite model of the sign.

3. Token/Type, Denotation/Designation

A particular occurrence of a sign – what Peirce labelled 'sinsign' (2:245) – is now more commonly called a *token*, whereas the class of all occurrences of the sign – Peirce's 'legisign' (8:363) – is called a *type*. Paraphrasing Peirce's own illustration, one can say that if a page in a book has 250 words upon it, this is the number of word tokens, whereas the number of different words on a page is the number of different word types (this distinction was also explored by Richards 1969).

Among the principal questions that have occupied most students of the verbal sign, three have seemed basic and inescapable: How do particular sign tokens *refer*? How do sign types acquire and maintain their constant capacity to *mean*? What precisely lies at the heart of the distinction between the relation of reference, or *denotation*, and the relation of meaning, or sense, or *designation*. A fourth question about the relation of meaning and use could also be added (Wells 1954). The modern cleavage between meaning and reference has recurred in many guises since Frege's classic consideration, in 1892, of *Sinn* and *Bedeutung* – Husserl's *Bedeutung* vs *Benutzung*, Mill's *denotation* vs *connotation*, Paul's *Bedenkung* vs *Benutzung*, Saussure's *valeur* vs *substance*. 'Semantics' is often, if loosely, used as a cover term encompassing both the theory of verbal reference and the theory of verbal meaning, but should, in the strict sense, be confined to the latter. Analytic philosophers, such as Carnap (1942), typically assign the theory of truth and the theory of logical deduction to semantics, on the ground that truth and logical consequence are concepts based on designation, and hence semantic concepts. The term *zoosemiotics* was coined in 1963 to extend the theory of meaning so as to account for presumably corresponding designative processes among the speechless creatures (Sebeok 1972a: 80).

A noticeable discrepancy between what a sign type designates and the denotation of one of its tokens may be responsible, on various levels, for the linguistic processes known to poetics and rhetoric as 'figures of speech,' as well as kindred phenomena found in animals (Bronowski 1967). This also underlies the mechanism involved in lying, which – certain opinions notwithstanding – corresponds to various forms of deception found throughout the animal kingdom.

Six Species of Signs

Recognition of the manifold possible relations between the two parts of a sign – the signifier and the signified – has led to numerous attempts by philosophers and philosophically inclined linguists, throughout the history of semiotics, to classify signs or systems of signs. Among these, Peirce's ultimate and maximal scheme – which he elaborated slowly but persistently over a period of some forty years – with sixty-six varieties, including intermediates and hybirds, was surely the most comprehensive, far-reaching, and subtle (Weiss and Burks 1945; but see Sanders 1970). In the verbal field, one of the more thoughtful and suggestive efforts of recent times was Bally's (1939), while Jakobson's (1970) special study devoted to the classification of human signs in general once again widens the horizons of current semiotic inquiry. Spang-Hanssen's (1954) survey provides a convenient overview of the psychological approaches of Ogden and Richards, Karl Britton, Bertrand Russell, and Charles Morris, as well as linguistic ones by scholars as heterogeneous as Ferdinand de Saussure, Leo Weisgerber, Alan H. Gardiner, Karl Bühler, Eric Buyssens, Leonard Bloomfield, and Louis Hjelmslev. Today, only some half a dozen species of signs – often with several more or less vaguely sense subspecies – are regularly identified and commonly employed, with but roughly comparable definitions; however, in virtually all cases, these are considered only over the domain of language and the human being's other species-specific systems, say, the secondary modelling systems of the Russian semiotic tradition that imply a verbal infrastructure, or music, or the like (Sebeok 1972a: 162–77). In what follows, the six species of signs that seem to occur most frequently in contemporary semiotics will be discussed, provisionally redefined, and illustrated not only from anthroposemiotic systems (i.e., those that are species-specific to humans), but also zoosemiotic systems, in order to show that none of the signs dealt with here is criterial of, or unique to, humans.

It should be clearly understood, finally, that it is not signs that are actually being classified, but more precisely, aspects of signs: in other words, a given sign may – and more often than not does – exhibit more than one aspect, so that one must recognize differences in gradation (Eco 1972a: 201). But it is equally important to grasp that the hierarchic principle is inherent in the architecture of any species of sign. For instance, a verbal symbol, such as an imperative, is commonly also endowed with a signal value. An emblem, which is a subspecies of symbol, may be partly iconic, such as the flag of the United States, since its seven red horizontal stripes alternating with six white ones stand for each founding colony, whereas its fifty white stars in the single blue canton correspond to each state in the Union. A primarily indexical sign, like a clock, acquires a discernible symbolic content in addition if the timepiece happens to be Big Ben. In the designs of the Australian Walbiri, the iconic bond between the forms of the sign vehicles and the referents assigned is said to be central, for, as Munn (1973: 177) points out, 'there is no systematic subordination of the iconic element to a second abstract ordering system,' in contrast to heraldry, where, as in a pictorial writing system, 'the iconic qualities linking the visual forms to their meanings tend to be attenuated,' that is, to become stepwise symbolic, 'because of the overall adjustment of the visual forms to another underlying sociocultural system for which the former constitutes a communication code.' (For the process of *deiconization*, see Wallis 1973: 487.) Morris's (1971: 191) dictum, 'Iconicity is ... a matter of degree,' coupled with Count's (1969: 102) comparably terse formula, 'Symbolization ... is supposable as a matter of a continuous (qualitative) degree,' seem to sum up the matter adequately.

To recapitulate, aspects of a sign necessarily co-occur in an environment-sensitive hierarchy. Since all signs, of course, enter into complex syntagmatic as well as paradigmatic contrasts and oppositions, it is their place both in the web of a concrete text and the network of an abstract system that is decisive as to which aspect will predominate in a given context at a particular moment, a fact which leads directly to the problem of levels, so familiar to linguistics – being an absolute prerequisite for any typology – but as yet far from developed in the other branches of semiotics. This important issue (see Lotman and Uspenskij 1973; Meletinsky and Segal 1971) can only be pointed out here. The sign is legitimately, if loosely, labelled after the aspect that ranks predominant.

Signal

The *signal* is a sign which mechanically (naturally) or conventionally (artificially) triggers some reaction on the part of a receiver. This is in accordance with the view that 'signals may ... be provided by nature, but they may also be produced artificially' (Kecskemeti 1952: 36). Note that the receiver can be either a machine or an organism, conceivably, even a personified supernatural (Sebeok 1972b: 514).

A most interesting and productive re-examination of the concept of signal is to be found in Pazukhin (1972). His argument and resultant definition, which resembles, but is not identical with, the one given above, rest on the development of a series of oppositions, stemming from the need to distinguish the physical, or technological, notion of signal from the one prevalent in the humanities and social sciences – briefly, from a purely semiotic conception; and the need, on the one hand, to separate physical phenomena which are signals from the class of non-signals, while, on the other hand, to discriminate signals from signs. It should be noted that Pazukhin wrenches Bühler's thesis out of its context and dismisses it out of hand as having given 'rise to numerous improper interpretations, which conceive Bühlerian signals as *species of signs* (*Zeichen*, after Bühler), conveying commands, requests and other kinds of imperative messages' (1972: 28). There are two fallacies involved here: one is the neglect of Bühler's so-called *organon* model as a whole, in which the concept of signal takes its logical place along with the concepts of symptom and symbol, and in isolation from which it cannot therefore be understood. A more serious error is to forget that one must constantly deal with *aspects* of signs: to repeat, a verbal command is very likely to have both a symbol-aspect and a signal-aspect, and the sign in question will oscillate between the two poles according to the context of its delivery.

It may be well to recall what Bühler did say about the signal within the framework of his model. In Bühler's view, the signal appeals to the destination, whose interior and exterior behaviour it governs; that is, it acts, as it were, like a traffic regulator, which elicits or inhibits reaction. By contrast, the symptom has to do with the source, whose inner behaviour it expresses; and the symbol relates to the designation (Bühler 1934: 28).

Pazukhin (1972: 29f.) rightly emphasizes the necessity 'to achieve a substantial discrimination of signals and signs,' and then analyses 'a few most promising tentatives,' including the hypotheses of such Russian philosophers or linguists as Abramian, Brudny, and Zalizniak, but finds fault with them all, chiefly owing to his conviction that none of them offers 'adequate criteria for a realistic opposition of signals to other media of interaction' (1972: 30). In my opinion, it is essential, first of all, to realize that the relation of signal to sign is that of a marked category to an unmarked one, that is, precisely that of a species to a genus to which it belongs, as Bühler also claimed. Secondly, Pazukhin introduces and discusses in detail what he calls two modes of control, both of which are interactions based on the idea of causal relationship: direct control and block-and-release control. Control by signalling is a special case of the latter, which naturally leads to the conclusion, implied by Pazukhin's (1972: 41) definition of signal, that there 'is only an occasional relationship between a signal and reactions produced by it.' This, however, is merely a weak echo of Peirce's explicit coupling of all sign-processes – hence signalling as well – with processes involving mediation or 'thirdness.' Witness the following passage:

It is important to understand what I mean by *semiosis*. All dynamical action, or action by brute force, physical or psychical, either takes place between two subjects ... or at any rate is a resultant of such actions between pairs. But by 'semiosis' I mean, on the contrary, an action, or influence, which is, or involves, a co-operation of *three* subjects, such as a sign, its object, and its interpretant, this tri-relative influence not being in any way resolvable into actions between pairs ... my definition confers on anything that so acts the title of a 'sign.' (Peirce 5:484)

Consider the following: C.R. Carpenter (1969: 44), a prominent student of animal behaviour, writing in connection with allopri-mates, takes the occasion to define signalling behaviour generally, in many qualities, forms, and patterns, as 'a condensed stimulus event, a part of a longer whole, which may arouse extended actions. Signaling activity, in its simplest form, is produced by an individual organism; it represents information; it is mediated by a physical carrier, and it is perceived and responded to by one or more individuals. Like the stimulus event, of which signalling behaviour is a special case, this kind of behaviour *releases* more energy than is used in signaling.' Now Pazukhin (1972: 41) rejects three criteria that have been variously proposed for defining sig-nals, on the ground that they 'cannot be considered essential.' These criteria – all of them used by Carpenter – are: the presence of a certain amount of energy; the delivery of information about something; and being dispatched by an animal. I completely endorse the elimination of all three factors from a viable definition of signal.

An example of a signal is the exclamation 'Go!' or, alternatively, the discharge of a pistol to start a footrace (a conventional releaser vs a mechanical trigger). The term is commonplace in studies of animal communication (Burkhardt 1967, Sebeok 1968, 1972a: 135–61), where it is often used interchangeably with a seldom defined zoosemiotic prime, *display* (e.g., Smith 1965: 405).

Symptom

A symptom is a compulsive, automatic, non-arbitrary sign, such that the signifier coupled with the signified in the manner of a natural link. A *syndrome* is a rule-governed configuration of symp-toms with a stable designatum. Both terms have strong, but not exclusively, medical connotations (Ostwald 1968); thus one can say, by metaphoric extension, 'the rise of modern anthropology was a symptom of colonialism,' and the like.

It is a peculiarity of symptoms that their denotata are generally different for the addresser (i.e., the patient – 'subjective symptoms') than for the addressee (i.e., the physician – 'objective symptoms'). In a felicitous phrase of Barthes (1972: 38), 'le symptôme, ce serait le réel apparent ou l'apparent réel' (for some Freudian implications of this observation see Brown 1958: 313 and Kecskemeti 1952: 61; and for semiotic work in this area see Shands 1970 and Ruesch 1973).

It is interesting to note that the subtle Port-Royal logicians drew a distinction between 'ordinary' symptoms and what physicians would call 'vital signs,' on the basis of an essentially quantitative criterion (Arnauld and Nicole 1816 [1662]). In other words, the specification 'compulsive, automatic' is subject to a probabilistic refinement for, although the denotation of a symptom is always equivalent to its cause in the source, some symptoms are effectively connected with an antecedent condition 'for sure,' whereas the link of other symptoms with the foregoing state of affairs is merely assumed with varying degrees of likelihood.

Semiotics – referring in earliest usage to medical concerns with the sensible indications of changes in the condition of the human body – constituted one of the three branches of Greek medicine. Since symptoms were among the earliest signs identified, they constitute a historically important category for any inquiry into the beginnings of the theory of signs, for instance, the thinking of such physicians as the Alexandrian physiologist Erasistratus (310–250 B.C.), the anatomist Herophilus (335–280 B.C.), and the Epicurean Asclepiades of Bithynnia (fl.110 B.C.), mentioned, among others, by Sextus Empiricus. Symptomatology, or *semeiology* (Sebeok 1973b), eventually developed into a branch of medicine with a specialized threefold preoccupation with diagnostics, focusing on the here and now, and its twin temporal projections into the anamnestic past and the prognostic future. A rapprochement between the general theory of, and the medical praxis involving, signs is rather recent, in no small way stimulated by the distinguished work of Michel Foucault (Barthes 1972: 38); but it was, in some measure, remarkably anticipated by Kleinpaul, in 1888, who paid homage to Hippocrates (460–377 B.C.) as the father and master of 'Semiotik' in having traced this nexus out in its Saussurean pre-figurements; and emphatically so by Crookshank (1925: 337–55).

Barthes (1972: 39), following Foucault, deems it wise to distinguish symptom from sign, and chooses to oppose the two within the well-known schema of Hjelmslev, whose elaboration on the bifacial character of the sign into form and substance, expression and content, seems to continue to fascinate Romance-language semioticians. Barthes assigns the symptom to the category that Hjelmslev called the substance of the signifier, and then goes on to argue that a symptom turns into a sign only when it enters in the context of clinical discourse, just when this transformation is wrought by the physician, in brief, solely 'par la médiation du langage.' However, such a view is tenable, if at all, only in such special cases when the destination of a symptomatic message is a physician or, by extension, a veterinarian, or at least a computer repair technician. In fact, the destination need be none of these; it could, for example, be a speechless creature. Autonomic effects, that is, symptomatic displays, were acutely observed and described by Darwin, and virtually all modern research in both interspecific and intraspecific animal communication ultimately rests on passages such as his remark that the erection of the dermal appendages, in a variety of vertebrates, 'is a reflex action, independent of the will; and this action must be looked at, when occurring under the influence of anger or fear, not as a power acquired for the sake of some advantage, but as an incidental result, at least to a large extent, of the sensorium being affected. The result, in as far as it is incidental, may be compared with the profuse sweating from an agony of pain or terror' in humans (Darwin 1872: 101). Human symptoms such as these, and a host of others, can easily be perceived and acted upon by such domesticated animals as dogs and horses (as the notorious Clever Hans episode in the history of psychology amply bears out, and for which see Hediger 1967), and in a variety of other situations in which language does not, indeed, cannot, play any sort of mediating role. In this global semiotic perspective, then, it remains my thesis that the opposition of symptom to sign parallels that of signal to sign, namely, of a marked category (species) to an unmarked one (genus).

It is likewise fallacious to assume that the function of a symptom is invariably morbific: as Kleinpaul (1972: 106) has astutely remarked, there must also exist a semiotic of 'radiant' good health, a condition where the organism may be observed, as it were, 'beaming' symptoms of well-being. Thus the exclusive identification of symptomatology with nosology can be quite misleading.

Note that Bühler (1934: fn.1) amplified his term 'Symptom' with two quasi-synonymous words, 'Anzeichen' and 'Indicum,' and that others would actually classify all symptoms as a subspecies of indexes, often with such qualifications as 'unwitting indexes' or 'mere unintended indexes' (Jakobson 1970: 10). The difficulty with this suggestion is that the place of 'intention' – or, more broadly, goal-orientation – in a communication model remains an entangled and controversial problem (Meiland 1970). In the sense of self-awareness – so-called 'subjective teleology' – the notion may be criterial in the definition of anthroposemiotic systems, and notably characterizes language, but it is hardly pertinent to zoosemiotic analysis, where introducing it may have stultifying effects. A more detailed discussion of intention lies beyond the scope of this chapter (see Sebeok 1973a).

Like all signs, symptoms may figure in both paradigmatic systems and syntagmatic chains. Investigation of the former role has hitherto been rudimentary, but it will become much better understood in this age of computer technology. A syntagmatic concate-nation of symptoms can be of two sorts: let us call them topical and temporal. A topical syntagm is made up of a bundle of symptoms manifested simultaneously, say, along different regions of a human body. Thus the basic operative parameters in a surgical procedure may involve an electrocardiogram, an electroencephalogram, cardiac output, central venous pressure, peripheral arterial pressure, rectal temperature, and respirations, all monitored and interpreted synchronously by the attendant medical team. A temporal syntagm implies input information from the same source, but at successive intervals set along the time axis. Thus Hediger (1968: 144) relates that the excrement of giraffes is kept under auditory observation in zoos as a continuing guide to the animal's state of health: 'normally, the falling of faeces should give a typical rustling sound,' he reports, but 'if the excrement is voided in shapeless, patterning portions,' the keeper is alerted to the possible existence of a pathological condition.

It might prove quite instructive to explore in much more depth such fruitful ideas as the interplay of paradigm and syntagm and of the axis of simultaneity with that of successivity, of substitution versus combination, and the like, in a field different from linguistics as (at first blush) symptomatology appears to be (Celan and Marcus 1973). Barthes's 1972 essay is suggestive, but essentially this task must await the considerable advancement of semiotics on a much broader front.

Icon

A sign is said to be iconic when there is a topological similarity between a signifier and its denotata. It was in 1867, in his paper 'On a New List of Categories,' that Peirce first published his now famous fundamental triad, and initially asserted that there were three kinds of signs (or, as he called them, 'representations'): (a) likenesses (a term he soon abandoned in favour of *icons*), or 'those whose relation to their objects is a mere community in some quality'; (b) *indices*, or 'those whose relation to their objects consists in a correspondence in fact'; and (c) *symbols* (which are the same as *general signs*), or 'those the ground of whose relation to their objects is an imputed quality,' which he later called 'laws,' meaning conventions, habits, or natural dispositions of its interpretant or of the field of its interpretant.

Peirce later distinguished three subclasses of icons: *images, diagrams*, and *metaphors*. The notion of the icon – which is ultimately related to the Platonic process of mimesis and which Aristotle then broadened from a chiefly visual representation to embrace all cognitive and epistemological experience – has been subjected to much analysis in its several varieties and manifestations, yet some seemingly intractable theoretical questions remain. Images (which are still sometimes simplistically equated with all icons, or worse, are naïvely assumed to be confined solely to the visual sphere) were studied in two exceptionally thoughtful inquiries by Eco (1972b) and by Wallis (1973) respectively. As for the theory of diagrams, this loomed very large in Peirce's own semiotic researches, and has been carefully reviewed by Zeman (1964) and Roberts (1973) in some of its far-reaching ramifications, which include modern graph theory. Peirce did not himself much pursue the ancient rhetorical device of metaphor, beyond correctly – notwithstanding Todorov's (1973: 17) stricture that the icon is a synecdoche rather than a metaphor – assigning this, in his list of categories, to the icon. The iconic functions of language have been studied in some detail (e.g., Jakobson 1965, Valesio 1969, Wescott 1971).

Despite the vast, ever multiplying, and by and large helpful literature advancing our understanding of the icon, several serious theoretical problems persist. Two among these – let us call them the issue of symmetry and the issue of regression – are worth at least a brief pause here; some others are discussed by Eco (1972a: 197–230, 1972b) in a consistently interesting albeit inconclusive way.

Wallis (1973: 482), for one, following custom, asserts *ex cathedra* that the 'relation of representation is nonsymmetrical: an iconic sign or an independent conventional sign represents its representatum but not vice versa.' Now let a snapshot of a reproduction of a famous painting – say, *La Gioconda* – be an iconic sign, or image, for the copy, which thus becomes the denotatum (or representatum), but which is itself an iconic sign for the original portrait hanging at the Louvre, its denotatum; but this painting, too, is an iconic sign for Leonardo's model, the lady known as Mona Lisa, *its* denotatum. In this diachronic sequence, Mona Lisa came first, her portrait next, then its reproduction, and finally a photograph of that. Note, however, that there is nothing in definitions of iconicity requiring the imposition of any kind of chronological priority: Peirce's definition speaks of 'a mere community in some quality,' and the one proposed at the start of this section only of 'a topological similarity,' both qualities which would apply backwards just as well as forwards. Is it merely an unmotivated convention to assign a progressive temporal sequence to the relation between signifier and signified? The difficulty can perhaps be driven home by way of the following: suppose a renowned contemporary personage, such as the pope, is known to me – as he is to most Catholics – only through his photograph, or some other pictorial representation, but that, one day, I get to see him in the flesh; on that occassion, the living pope would become for me the 'iconic sign' for his long-familiar image, its photographic or lithographic denotatum. This problem is not unfamiliar to ethologists either. Thus Lorenz (Introduction to Wickler 1968: xi) alluded to this in his remark that the 'form of the horse's hoof is just as much an image of the steppe it treads as the impression it leaves is an image of the hoof.' If this attribute of reflexivity can be shown to be an indispensable characteristic property of icons, then surely time's arrow must be incorporated in revisions of extant definitions.

As for the vertiginous problem of regression, let it be illustrated by the following: an infant daughter can be said to be an iconic sign for her mother if there is a topological similarity between her, as signifier, and her mother, its denotatum; however, the little girl can likewise, though doubtless to a lesser degree, stand as an iconic sign for her father, every one of her siblings, all of her kinfolk, and, further still, all mammals, all vertebrates, and so forth, and so on, in unending retrogression to ever more generalized denotata.

There are many instances of iconicity in animal discourse (Sebeok 1968: 614ff.), involving virtually all of the available channels – chemical, auditory, or visual. The iconic function of a chemical sign is well illustrated by the alarm substance of the ant *Pogonomyrmex badius*: if the danger to the colony is momentary, the signal – a quantum of released pheromone – quickly fades and leaves the bulk of the colony undisturbed; conversely, if it persists, the substance spreads, involving an ever-increasing number of workers. The sign is iconic inasmuch as it varies in analogous proportion to the waxing or waning of the danger stimuli (Sebeok 1972a: 95f.).

The behaviour of certain vespine audio-mimics illustrates the iconic function of an auditory sign. Thus the fly *Spilomyia hamifera* Lw. displays a wing-beat rate of 147 strokes per second while hovering near the wasp *Dolichovespula arenaria* F. (which it closely resembles in colour pattern). Since this wasp flies with 1250 wing strokes per second, the two flight sounds are presumed to be indistinguishable to predators, and fly-catching birds are thus deceived (Sebeok 1972a: 86f.).

Finally, an elegant (if sometimes disputed) example of a complex piece of behaviour that evolved, as it were, to function as a visual iconic sign is graphically described by Kloft (1959): the hind end of an aphid's abdomen, and the kicking of its hind legs, constitute, for an ant worker, a compound sign vehicle, signifying the head of another ant together with its antennal movement. In other words, the ant is alleged to identify likeness (the near end of the aphid) with its denotatum (the front end of an ant) and act on this information, that is, treat the aphid in the manner of an *effigy* (a subspecies of icon).

Index

A sign is said to be indexic insofar as its signifier is contiguous with its signified, or is a sample of it. The term *contiguous* is not to be interpreted literally in this definition as necessarily meaning 'adjoining' or 'adjacent': thus Polaris may be considered an index of the north celestial pole to any earthling, in spite of the immense distances involved. Rather, continuity should be thought of in classical juxtaposition to the key principle in the definition of the icon, to wit, similarity. 'Contiguous' was chosen because of its pervasive use, when paired with 'similar,' in many fields of intellectual endeavour, ranging from homeopathic versus contagious magic to poetics and rhetoric (system vs text, metaphor vs metonym), *Gestalt* psychology (factor of similarity vs factor of proximity [Wertheimer 1923: 304–11]), neurology (hypothesis of the polar types of aphasia by Jakobson and Luria), and, of course, linguistics in the Saussurean tradition (paradigmatic axis vs syntagmatic axis, opposition vs contrast), etc.

Peirce's notion of the index was at once novel and fruitful, as Wells (1967) has rightly emphasized. His indexical signs have received close study by some of the most prominent philosophers of our time, whether they tagged them egocentric particulars (Russell 1940), token-reflexive words (Reichenbach 1948), indexical expressions (Bar-Hillel 1954), or something else (Gale 1967). At the same time, Peirce's ideas have informed the views of some linguists, to the effect that grammatical theory 'must take into its scope ... a theory of conversation, and [that] certain understandings about deixis and pronominal reference make up part of that theory' (Fillmore 1972: 275). Deixis is a well-known phenomenon to linguists (Frei 1944, Bursill-Hill 1963), notably in the guise of the 'shifter' – a mot juste coined by Jespersen in 1922 (1964), whose idea was extended, among others, by Sturtevant (1947: 135f.), Jakobson (1963), and especially Fillmore (1973) in his admirable series of papers devoted to the spatial, temporal, discourse-oriented, and social deictic anchoring of utterances in 'the real world.'

In one of his most memorable examples, Peirce recalls that the footprint Robinson Crusoe found in the sand was an index to him of some creature. In like fashion, a vast map of such records is printed overnight by animals of all sorts, all over the countryside, leaving tracks and traces 'of immense variety, often of wonderful clarity.' These 'stories written in footprint code' compel 'countryside detection' and have been beautifully deciphered by such experienced field naturalists as Ennion and Tinbergen (1967: 5); their meticulous track photographs and prints depict an astonishing array of indexical signs in the most literal and immediate sense.

The pointed lip gesture in use among the Cuna Indians of Panama, as analysed by Sherzer (1973), provides a neat instance of cultural integration into a single unified arrangement of a verbal index with a non-verbal index. His description also shows that, whereas the index constitutes a marked category in opposition to the sign, the Cuna lip work stays unmarked in its focal indexical function in opposition to those accretive forms that have acquired peripheral meanings.

A small family of cerophagous picarian birds, a common species of which bears the scientific name *Indicator indicator* (*nomen est omen?*), are the celebrated honey-guides. These birds have developed a remarkable symbiotic relationship with certain mammals – ratels, baboons, and humans – by employment of a purely indexical link: they guide their symbionts to the vicinity of wild bees' nests. The leading is preponderantly delophonic, but delotropic elements enter into it too: a would-be guiding bird will come to, say, a person and chatter until followed, but keep out of sight of the pursuer most of the time. Although its dipping flight is conspicuous, with the bird's white tail feathers widely spread, the honey guide 'indicates' mainly by means of a repetitive series of chirring notes that subside only when it sees or hears flying, buzzing bees, whose nests, of course, are the target (Friedmann 1955).

The theory of honey-bee (*Apis mellifera*) exploitation of food sources has been described (Frisch 1967) and pondered by many scientists, including semioticians and linguists. It is common knowledge that if the food source is farther away than a hundred metres, the tail-wagging dance conveys, among other bits of information, the direction of the goal, the sun being used as the reference point. Now if the bee dances on a horizontal surface, 'the direction of a waggling run points directly to the goal,' that is to say, the sign is indexical (the rhythm 'indicates' the distance in analog fashion: the farther away the goal, the fewer cycles of the dance in a given time). If, however, the dance takes place on a vertical comb surface – as is the case, as a rule, in the dark hive – then 'the dancer transposes the solar angle into the gravitational angle' (if the run is pointed upward, this indicates that the food source lies in the direction of the sun, if downwards, opposite the sun, if 60° left of straight up, 60° to the left of the sun, and so forth) (Frisch 1967: 230f.). If a vertical honeycomb is involved, in other words, when an angle with respect to gravity is used as the orientation cue, the sign ceases to be an index: its symbolic aspect now ranks predominant.

Symbol

A sign without either similarity or contiguity, but only with a conventional link between its signifier and its denotata, and with an intentional class for its designatum, is called a symbol. The feature 'conventional link' – Peirce's 'imputed character' – is introduced, of course, to distinguish the symbol from both the icon and the index, while the feature 'intension' is required to distinguish it from the name. The logical opposition between intension (sometimes also called 'objective intension,' and often 'comprehension') and extension has been drawn in a bewildering number and variety of ways – from 530 B.C. to the present (Carnap 1956: 18, Stanosz 1970). For the present purposes, an intensionally defined class is one defined by the use of a propositional function; the denotata of the designation are defined in terms of properties shared by, and only by, all the members of that class, whether these properties are known or not (Reichenbach 1948: 193). In the terminology of Lewis (1946: 39), intension refers to 'the conjunction of all terms each of which must be applicable to anything to which the given term would be applicable.'

Admittedly, 'symbol' is the most abused term of those under consideration here. In consequence, it has either tended to be grotesquely overburdened, or, on the contrary, reduced to more general kinds of behavioural phenomena, or even to absurd nullity. A few brief illustrative instances of both tendencies will suffice here; they are merely intended to underline the need for further conceptual clarification.

An unjustifiably excessive generalization and overly broad application of the concept of symbolic forms mark the writings of many of Ernst Cassirer's epigones or of those indirectly influenced by his philosophy (Sebeok 1973a: 189). In cultural anthropology, a case in point is Leslie White (1940: 454), who once wrote: 'Human behavior is symbolic behavior; symbolic behavior is human behavior. The symbol is the universe of humanity ... the key to this world and the means of participation in it is – the symbol.' This hyperbole was reflected, essentially, in the viewpoint espoused by the founder of the International Society for the Study of Symbols and so advocated by him (Kahn 1969).

According to the psychologist Kantor (1936: 63), 'the term symbol is made to do duty for everything the psychologist calls a stimulus.' One may well ask, how widespread is the redundancy among cognitive scientists?

Although the term is included in Cherry's (1966: 309) otherwise helpful glossary, it is immediately followed by this odd disclaimer: 'We avoid the term *symbol* as far as possible in this book.' As a matter of fact, linguists have always tended to shy away from the term with only a few exceptions (e.g., Landar 1966, Chao 1968).

A number of important symbol subspecies – whose semiotic import, however, has seldom been properly analysed – are in more or less common use, at least in contemporary English. Such subordinate terms, with increasing intension, include: *allegory, badge, brand, device* (in heraldry), *emblem, insignia, mark,* and *stigma* (when not embodied as a symptom, as in the expression 'venous stigmata,' suggesting alcoholic excess) (Goffman 1963: 1–2).

Let us take a brief look at only one of these – the *emblem.* It is clear, from the outset, that its distribution must be narrower than that of its immediate superordinate: thus, one can say that the hammer and sickle was either the symbol or the emblem of the Communist Party, or the Eiffel Tower of Paris, but one cannot say that H_2O is a *chemical emblem.*

Following a proposal put forward by David Efron in 1941 (1972), Ekman and Friesen (1969: 59) reintroduced and sharpened the notion of the emblem:

Emblems differ from most other nonverbal behaviors primarily in their usage, and in particular in their relationship to verbal behavior, awareness and intentionality. Emblems are those nonverbal acts which have a direct verbal translation, or dictionary definition, usually consisting of a word or two, or perhaps a phrase. This verbal definition or translation of the emblem is well known by all members of a group, class, or culture ... People are almost always aware of their use of emblems; that is, they know when they are using an emblem, can repeat it if asked to do so, and will take communicational responsibility for it.

They have in mind here the nonverbal emblems only, and it is, indeed, the case that an emblem is most often conceived of as a highly formalized symbol in the visual modality. However, this need not always be so. Thus Lévi-Strauss has suggested (in a personal communication) that recited genealogies of notable individuals, say, of African ancestor chiefs, may well be regarded as being emblematic; such verbal acts could readily be accommodated within the scope of the foregoing formulation, as perhaps could Hollander's (1959) decidedly more idiosyncratic usage in connection with metrics.

It should be obvious, even from these sparse paragraphs, that the *Wortfeld* of the symbol is a very complex one indeed, and that the emblem and its congeners must await a fully correct lexicographic domain of the immediately dominant term, symbol, as a whole.

Symbols are often asserted to be the exclusive property of human beings, but the capacity of organisms to form intentional class concepts obtains far down in phylogenesis (Jacob 1974: 319), and the ability for constructing universals from particulars was provided with a solid mathematical-neurological rationalization by Pitts and McCulloch (1947, see Arbib 1971). According to both the definition of the symbol offered here and the more common Aristotelian definitions resting on the doctrine of arbitrariness that were promoted in linguistics, especially by Whitney and Saussure (Engler 1962, Coseriu 1967), animals undoubtedly do have symbols. I have previously commented on the arbitrariness of tail work in dogs, cats, and horses (Haldane 1955: 387, Sebeok 1973a: 196), a set of examples that could easily be amplified: thus a fearful rhesus monkey carries its tail stiffly out behind, whereas, in baboons, fear is conveyed by a vertical tail. However, the converse is not necessarily true: 'a mother of a young infant [baboon] may hold her tail vertical not in fear but to help her infant balance on her back; and the tail may also be held vertical while its owner is being groomed in the tail region' (Rowell 1972: 87). According to Altmann (1967: 376), with 'few exceptions, the semantic social signals that have been studied in primates so far are arbitrary representations'; and, more, generally, according to Bronowski (1967: 376), it 'might be thought that because only human beings think with arbitrary symbols, they are also alone in speaking with them. But once again, this is not so' (see also Malson 1973 and Lurker 1968: 4).

For one more example of a symbol in animal behaviour, I turn to the insects of the carnivorous family *Empididae*. In a species of dipterans of this family, the male offers the female an empty balloon prior to copulation. The evolutionary origin, that is, the increasing ritualization (Huxley 1966), of this seemingly bizarre gesture has been unravelled step by step by biologists, but this story is irrelevant in synchronic perspective: the fact is that the gift of an empty balloon is a wholly arbitrary sign, the transfer of which simply reduces the probability that the male himself will fall prey to his female partner.

Name

A sign which has an extensional class for its designatum is called a name. In accordance with this definition, individuals denoted by a proper name such as *Veronica* have no common property attributed to them save the fact that they all answer to 'Veronica.' An extensional definition of a class is one that is given 'by listing the names of the members, or by pointing to every member successively' (Reichenbach 1948: 193); or, as Kecskemeti (1952: 130) put it, 'considered in terms of its intension ... a name is simply a blank, unless and until a description referring to the same object is supplied,' say, 'Veronica with the handkerchief,' Saint Veronica, or the like (see also Sørenson 1963).

When the signification of a sign permits only one denotatum it is said to be singular. Singular signs, including proper names, belong to a mode of signifying that Morris (1971: 76f.) has labelled *namors*, 'which are language symbols.' Namors are members of the same family of signs, called 'identifiors,' to which two other subcategories belong: *indicators*, the non-linguistic pendant to namors; and *descriptors*, 'identifiors which describe a location.' In the parlance of Husserl (1970: 341f.), the name of a person is also normally univocal (*eindeutig*) although it may, by chance, be plurivocal (*mehrdeutig*). Human individuals are identified by verbally attestable namors, say, a personal name or (in the United States since 1935) a unique social security registration number; and by a host of non-verbal indicators, 'the means by which a person, or dead body, may be definitely recognized, even in cases where the person purposely attempts to mislead' (Wilder and Wentworth 1918: 5).

It is well known that all animals broadcast a steady stream of 'indentifiors,' that is, displays identifying their source in one or more ways: as to species, reproductive status, location in space or time, rank in a social hierarchy, momentary mood, and the like (Sebeok 1972a: 130). In addition, the best organized societies of vertebrates can be distinguished by a single trait so overriding in its consequences that the other characteristics seem to flow from it. Wilson (1971: 402) remarks, as he draws a pivotal distinction between the impersonal societies formed by the insects, on the one hand, and the 'personal' societies found in birds and mammals on the other: this attribute is the recognition of individual identity, a feature of relatively small circles with long-term socialization in the young that presupposes play and has as its corollary a high degree of mutual cooperation among adults. Each member of such a society 'bears some particular relationship to every other member' and thereby comes to be known to all others as unique. Coupled to efforts to establish and maintain the requisite network of multifarious 'personal' bonds is the development of an intimate form of communication, which necessarily involves the use of appropriate supportive signs: thus the notion of 'uniqueness' implies the manifestation of indicators, or, in Goffman's (1963: 56) terminology, 'identity pegs.'

The literature on vertebrate communication takes it for granted – at least *ex hypothesi* – that indicators (i.e., their own names) are universally incorporated into all messages of birds and mammals (Smith 1969a, 1969b). Thorpe.(1967) has shown that when a partner is absent, the remaining bird will use the sounds normally reserved for the partner, with the result that the said partner will return as quickly as possible as if called by name. Specific examples can be multiplied from a variety of vertebrates, including canines and felines, primates (Lawick-Goodall 1968, Rowell 1972), and marine mammals. Individual whale click trains are even referred to as 'signatures' (Backus and Schevill 1966), apparently by analogy with the so-called 'signature-tunes' of birds.

On the Being, Behaving, and Becoming of Signs

This chapter has dealt with a half dozen possible relationships that are empirically found to prevail between the signifier and the signified components of signs, and certain problems attendant to the definitions offered, in particular as these may have a bearing on their classification. The discussion has been concerned with the *being* of a sign, or its structure, that is, its enduring status in a synchronic sense; the focus of the inquiry fell within the realm of signification. A structural definition of the sign is analytic, intrinsic, and static; it utilizes types of associations inherent, in fact or virtually, in the architecture of the sign itself.

It should be supplemented, however, with a searching examination of the sign's *behaving*, or its function, a repetitive perturbation along a secular trend. A functional definition of the sign is pragmatic, extrinsic, but dynamic; it is based upon variations at different nodal points of an expanded model of the communicative process, as depicted, for instance by a Morley triangle (Sebeok 1972a: 14). Wells (1967: 103) has aptly stated that 'semiotics has two groups of affinities. It is concerned, on the one hand, with communication, and, on the other, with meaning.'

The question of *becoming*, or history, representing cumulative changes in the longitudinal time section, introduces manifold diachronic considerations. These are of two rather different sorts: those having to do with the evolution of signs in phylogeny, in a word, their ritualization (Huxley 1966); and those having to do with their elaboration in ontogeny. Study of the former requires the collaboration of ethology with semiotics; research of the latter belongs to the advancing field of psycholinguistics.

In sum, although semiotics is most commonly regarded as a branch of the communication disciplines, the criteria that must be integrated when working toward even a reasonably holistic comprehension of signs derive from studies of both signification and communication (*noumena* and *phenomena*), and they must also be in good conformity with research findings in ethology and developmental psychology.

Applying the Law of Inverse Variation

The terms *sign, symbol, emblem,* and *insignia* are here arranged in the order of their subordination, each term to the left being a genus of its subclass to the right, and each term to the right being a species of its genus to the left. Thus the denotation of these terms decreases: for example, the extension of 'symbol' includes the extension of 'emblem,' but not conversely. As well, the conventional intension of each term increases: the intension of 'emblem' includes the intension of 'symbol.' Sometimes, however, variation in the intension is accompanied by no change in the extension: thus, in the sequence 'sign,' 'symbol,' 'omen,' 'augury,' and 'portent' the extension of the last pair of terms is, within the semiotic universe of discourse, materially the same. This implies that if a series of semiotic categories is arranged in order of their increasing intension, the denotation of the terms will either diminish or will remain the same.

A Lexical Domain

Besides the six species of signs described here, allusion has been made to a wide variety of others, including allegory, badge, brand, descriptor, device, diagram, display, effigy, emblem, identifior, identity peg, image indicator, insignia, mark, metaphor, namor, signature, stigma, and syndrome. No doubt, these and a high number of cognate terms – especially those introduced by Peirce (2:254–63) and Morris (1971: 20–3) – would need a separate treatment, despite Revzina's (1972: 231) remark that it would evidently be more natural to treat the definitions of signs 'as an attempt at a lexicographical interpretation of corresponding language concepts.'

The Ubiquity of Signs

As the English zoologist R.J. Pumphrey pointed out, there are two schools of thought with regard to language development (see Sebeok 1972a: 88). One claims that human speech is different in material particulars from that of other animals, but that the two are tied by evolution (continuity theory). The other claims that speech is a specifically human attribute, a function *de novo*, different in kind from anything of which other animals are capable (discontinuity theory). Without supporting one or the other, one thing must, above all else, be emphasized: it is essential to adopt a research strategy that compares human and animal communication systems in order to get a meaningful glimpse into the nature and ubiquity of semiosis.

4

Symptom Signs

In the previous chapter it was pointed out that the symptom was a rudimentary sign connected intrinsically with bodily processes. Symptoms were the first signs examined by the medical practitioners of the ancient world; and their study led to the foundation of semiotics as a branch of medical science. In this chapter, I will look more closely at symptom signs.

Ullmann (1951: 161) distinguished among four juxtaposed branches of word study: '(1) the science of names (lexicology if synchronistic, etymology if diachronistic); (2) the science of meanings (semantics); (3) the science of designations (onomasiology); (4) the science of concepts (*Begriffslehre*).' Although the distinction between designation and meaning is far from consistently drawn or pellucid, I take it that this alterity depends on whether one's starting point is the *name*, the *lexeme*, or, more generally, the *sign*; or whether it is the *concept* or, more generally, the *object*, that is, the constellation of properties and relations the sign stands for. If the former, the analysis should yield a semiotic network responsive to the question, What does a given sign signify in contrast and opposition to any other sign within the same system of signs? If the latter, the analysis should reveal the sign by which a given entity is designated within a certain semiotic system. According to Ullmann, the second inquiry is the cornerstone of the distinction, but I believe that the two questions are indissolubly complementary. In any case, the whole enterprise critically hinges upon how the investigator parses the sign/object (*aliquid/aliquo*) antithesis, and what the conjunctive *stands for*, in the judgment of the investigator, entails.

The probe becomes at once more intricate, but also more intriguing, when the lexical field (*Bedeutungsfeld? Sinnfeld? Wortfeld?*) being explored happens to be reflexive, that is, self-searching. Such is the case of symptom signs. An examination of this sign type may begin in the inner realm of the lexicon, if viewed as a name, or in the outer realm of clinical experience, if viewed as sense.

The Meaning of Symptom

One may properly inquire: what does the lexeme *symptom* mean in a certain language; or what does the same lexeme designate, that is, reveal as a diagnostic intimation, with respect to, say, an actual quality of 'diseasehood' (Fabrega 1974: 123) that Crookshank (in Ogden and Richards 1923: 343) foresightedly portrayed as 'a mysterious *substantia* that has biological properties and produces symptoms'? In the end, the results of such dichotomous inquiries amalgamate in a common dialectical synthesis. For the present purposes, the language chosen is American English. However, the semantic field of 'medical discourse,' which is typically nested within wider sets of concentric frames (Labov and Fanshel 1977: 36f.), is here assumed to be, *mutatis mutandis*, very similar to that in every other speech community committed to the paradigm of medical theory and practice 'in the context of the great tradition' (Miller 1978: 184) of thinking marked by a continuity that links modern clinicians with the idea of insomnia launched by the brilliant Alcmaeon of Croton during the first half of the fifth century B.C. This heritage was further consolidated by Hippocrates – arguably considered, at one and the same time, the 'father of medicine' (Heidel 1941: xiii), and the 'father and master of semiotics' (Kleinpaul 1972: 103) – then Plato, Aristotle, and the Alexandrian physicians of the fourth century B.C. Equally perceptive studies of *symptom* have, in fact, cropped up in the semiotic literature (e.g., Baer 1982) and in the medical literature (e.g., Prodi 1981), undertaken by savants who mutually know their way around the other field as well as their own (see also Staiano 1979). One should, however, continue to be ever mindful of the admonition of Mounin

(1981) against a mechanical application of semiotic (especially linguistic) concepts to medicine (especially psychiatry).

Symptom always appears in conjunction with *sign,* but the precise
nature of the vinculum is far from obvious (as in MacBryde and
Blacklow 1970 or Chamberlain and Ogilvie 1974). The basic semiosic facts were perspicuously depicted by Ogden and Richards
(1923: 21):

If we stand in the neighbourhood of a crossroad and observe a pedestrian
confronted by a notice To *Grandchester* displayed on a post, we commonly
distinguish three important factors in the situation. There is, we are sure,
(1) a Sign which (2) refers to a Place and (3) is being inter-preted by a
person. All situations in which Signs are considered are similar to this.
A doctor noting that his patient has a temperature and so forth is said to
diagnose his disease as influenza. If we talk like this we do not make it
clear that signs are here also involved. Even when we speak of symptoms
we often do not think of these as closely related to other groups of signs.
But if we say that the doctor interprets the tem-perature, etc. as a Sign of
influenza, we are at any rate on the way to an inquiry as to whether there
is anything in common between the manner in which the pedestrian
treated the object at the crossroad and that in which the doctor treated
his thermometer and the flushed countenance.

The relation of sign to symptom involves either coordination or
subordination. If the distinction is between coordinates, what mat-
ters is not their inherent meaning but the mere fact of the binary
opposition between the paired categories. This was nicely brought
to the fore in a report of an investigation of the symptom 'fatigue'
by two physicians, Shands and Finesinger (Shands 1970: 52):

The close study of ... patients made it imperative to differentiate carefully
between 'fatigue,' a feeling, and 'impairment,' an observable decrement
in performance following protracted effort. The distinction comes to be
that between a *symptom* and a *sign*. The symptom is felt, the sign observed
by some other person. These two terms cover the broad field of semiotics; they are often confused, and the terms interchanged without
warning.

This passage underscores the importance of separating the 'private world' of introspection reported by the description of the symptoms on the part of the patient from the public world of signs reported by the description of behaviour on the part of the physician. As pointed out elsewhere: 'It is a peculiarity of symptoms that their denotata are generally different from the addresser, i.e. the patient ("subjective symptoms," confusingly called by many medical practitioners "signs") and the addressee, i.e. the examining physician ("objective symptoms," or simply "symptoms")' (Sebeok 1976: 181). Note that only a single observer – to wit, oneself – can relate symptomatic events, whereas an indefinite number of observers – including oneself – can observe signs. Accordingly, within this framework the fact of privacy looms as a criterial distinctive feature that demarcates any symptom from any sign (Sebeok 1979). Symptoms could thus be read as recondite communiqués about an individual's inner world, an interpretation that sometimes acquires that status of an elaborate occult metaphor. For instance, the eating disorder anorexia nervosa would appear to be reasonably decodable as 'I am starving (emotionally) to death.' Its symptoms are believed to result from disturbed family relationships and interpersonal difficulties (Liebman, Minuchin, and Baker 1974a, 1974b). One palpable sign of this ailment is, of course, weight phobia, measurable as a decrement in the patient's mass.

The crucial distinction between fatigue and impairment is similar to that between anxiety as a felt symptom and behavioural disintegration often exhibited in states of panic. The latter is a sign, not a symptom (Shands 1970). The dissemblance exemplified here is obviously related to Uexküll's (1982: 209) notion, maintained both in the life and the sign sciences of 'inside' and 'outside.' I take the pivotal implication of this to be as follows: 'Something observed (= outside) stands for something that is (hypothetically) noticed by the observed subjects (= inside). Or something within the observing system stands for something within the observed system' (Uexküll 1982: 209). For any communication, this complementary relationship is obligatory, because the organism and its *Umwelt* together constitute a system. The shift from physiological process to semiosis is a consequence of the fact that the observer assumes a hypothetical stance within the observed system (*Bedeutungsertei-lung–Bedeutungsverwertung*).

For *symptom*, there exists an array of both stricter and looser synonyms. Among the former, which appear to be more or less commonly employed, Elstein et al. (1978: 279) solely and extensively use *cue*. Although they do so without a definition, their import is made quite clear from passages such as 'cues were interpreted by physicians as tending to confirm or disconfirm a hypothesis, or as noncontributory.' Fabrega (1974: 126) seems to prefer *indicator*, but he uses this commutably for either *symptom* or *sign*; and when he remarks that 'all indicators may be needed in order to make judgments about disease,' he surely refers to both categories together. The word *clue*, however, is a looser synonym for *symptom*: generally speaking, whereas *symptom* is used in medical discourse, *clue* is found in the detective sphere (Sebeok 1981a, Eco and Sebeok 1983).

In the minimalist coupling, *sign* and *symptom* are equipollent; both are unmarked vis-à-vis one another (Waugh 1982). Sometimes, however, *symptom* encompasses both 'the objective sign and the subjective sign' (Staiano 1982: 332). In another tradition, *symptom* is a mere phenomenon 'qui précisément n'a encore rien de sémiologique, de sémantique,' or is considered falling (e.g., in the terminology of glossematics) in the area of content articulation, *la substance du signifiant*, an operationally designated *figura* that is elevated to full semiotic status only through the organizing consciousness of the physician, achieved through the mediation of language (Barthes 1972: 38f.). However, still other radically different sorts of arrangements occur in the literature. In Bühler's *organon* model (see Sebeok 1981b), *symptom* constitutes but one of three 'variable moments' capable of rising 'in three different ways to the rank of a sign.' These include *signal*, *symbol*, as well as *symptom*. Bühler (1934: 28) specifies further that the semantic relation of the latter functions 'by reason of its dependence on the sender, whose interiority it expresses.' He clearly subordinates this trio of words under one and the same *Oberbegriff Zeichen*. It should also be noted that Bühler's first mention of *symptom* is immediately followed by a parenthetic set of presumed synonyms: *Anzeichen*, *Indicium*. Thus, in acknowledging the importance of the notion of privacy as an essential unmarked feature of *symptom*, Bühler also recognizes that, while it is coordinate with two other terms, it is also subordinate to the (unmarked) generic notion of *sign*, namely that kind of sign that Peirce earlier, but unbeknownst to Bühler, defined with much more exactitude as an *index*.

The Peircean View

Despite his extensive knowledge of medicine (Sebeok 1981a), Peirce did not often discuss *symptom* (nor anywhere, in any fecund way, *syndrome*, *diagnosis*, *prognosis*, or the like). For him, a *symptom*, to begin with, was one kind of sign. In a very interesting passage, from the dictionary lemma 'Represent,' he expands: 'to stand for, that is, to be in such a relation to another that for certain purposes it is treated by some mind as if it were that other. Thus, a spokesman, deputy, attorney, agent, vicar, diagram, symptom, counter, description, concept, premise, testimony, all represent something else, in their several ways, to minds who consider them in that way' (Peirce 2:273).

For Peirce, however, a symptom was never a distinct species of sign, but a mere subspecies, namely the index – or secondness of genuine degree (in contrast to a demonstrative pronoun, exemplifying secondness of a degenerative nature) – of one of his three canonical categories. But what kind of sign is this? Peirce (2:304) gives an example that I would prefer to label a *clue*: 'Such for instance, is a piece of mould with a bullet-hole in it as a sign of a shot; for without a shot there would have been no hole; but there is a hole there, whether anybody has the sense to attribute it to a shot or not.' The essential point here is that the indexical character of the sign would not be voided if there were no interpretant, but only if its object was removed. An index is that kind of a sign that becomes such by virtue of being really (i.e., factually) connected with its object: 'such is a symptom of disease' (Peirce 8:119). All 'symptoms of disease,' furthermore, 'have no utterer,' as is also the case with 'signs of the weather' (8:185). We have an index, Peirce prescribed in 1885, when there is 'a direct dual relation of the sign to its object independent of the mind using the sign ... Of this nature are all natural signs and physical symptoms' (3:361).

A further detail worth pointing out is that Peirce calls the 'occurrence of a symptom of a disease ... a legisign, a general type of a definite character,' but 'the occurrence in a particular case is a sinsign' (8:335), that is to say, a token. A somewhat cryptic remark reinforces this: 'To a sign which gives reason to think that something is true, I prefer to give the name of a *symbol*; although the words *token* and *symptom* likewise recommend themselves.' Staiano (1982: 331) is undoubtedly correct in remarking that 'the appearance of a symptom in an individual is thus an indexical sinsign, while the symptom interpreted apart from its manifestation becomes an indexical legisign.'

Symptoms, in Peirce's usage, are thus unwitting indexes, interpretable by their receivers without the actuality of any intentional sender. Jakobson (1971: 703) likewise includes symptoms within the scope of semiotics but cautions that 'we must consistently take into account the decisive difference between communication which implies a real or alleged addresser and information whose source cannot be viewed an addresser by the interpreter of the indications obtained.' This remark glosses over the fact that symptoms are promptings of the body crying out for an explanation – for the construction, by the self, of a coherent and intelligible pattern (which of course may or may not be accurate, for which see Polunin 1977: 91). Pain comprises one such symptom that embodies a message compelling the central nervous system to influence both covert and overt behaviour to seek out signs of pain, throughout phylogeny, ontogeny *hic et ubique*. Miller (1978: 45–9) befittingly expands:

From the instant when someone first recognizes his symptoms to the moment when he eventually complains about them, there is always an interval, longer or shorter as the case may be, when he argues with himself about whether it is worth making a complaint known to an expert ... At one time or another we have all been irked by aches and pains. We have probably noticed alterations in weight, complexion and bodily function, changes in power, capability and will, unaccountable shifts of mood. But on the whole we treat these like changes in the weather.

As pointed out in the previous chapter, Peirce (4:351) once particularized the footprint Robinson Crusoe found in the sand to be an index 'that some creature was on his island'; and indeed an index always performs as a sign the vectorial direction of which is toward the past, or, as Thom (1980: 194) put it, 'par réversion de la causalité génératrice,' which is the inverse of physical causality. Augustine's class of *signa naturali*, defined – in contrast to *signa data* – by the relation of dependence between sign and the things signified (*De Doctrina Christiana* 2.1.2), besides its orthodox sense (such as a rash as a symptom of measles), is also illustrated by footprints left by an animal passed out of sight, and may thus be regarded as encompassing a portent, or in the most general usage, evidence (for instance, as a southwesterly wind may both signify and bring rain; i.e., give rise to its significatum). Thus symptoms, in many respects, function like tracks – footprints, toothmarks, food pellets, droppings and urine, paths and runs, snapped twigs, lairs, the remains of meals, etc. – throughout the animal world (Sebeok 1976: 133) and in hunting populations in which humans 'learnt to sniff, to observe, to give meaning and context to the slightest trace' (Ginzburg 1983). Tracks, including notably symptoms, operate like metonyms. This trope is also involved in *pars pro toto*, as extensively analysed by Bilz (1940).

Symptoms and the Medical Origins of Semiotics

It is, of course, Hippocrates who remains the emblematic ancestral figure of semiotics – that is, of semiology, in the narrow sense of symptomatology – although he 'took the notion of clue from the physicians who came before him' (Eco 1980: 277). Baer (1982: 18) alludes to a 'romantic symptomatology,' which he postulates may have been 'the original one,' carrying the field back 'to an era of mythical consciousness.' Alcmaeon remarked, in one of the scanty fragments of his book: 'As to things invisible and things mortal, the gods have certainties; but, so far as men may infer ... men must proceed by clues' (Eco 1980: 281), namely 'provisional conjecture.' And what is to be the basis of such circumstantial inference? Clearly, the concept that has always been central is *symptom* (Ginzburg 1983).

While Alcmaeon is commonly regarded as the founder of empirical psychology, it was Hippocrates, a clinical teacher *par excellence* (Temkin 1973), who broke with archaic medical practice, in which the physician was typically preoccupied with the nature of the disease, its causes and manifestations, and refocused directly upon the sick person and his/her complaints – in brief, upon the *symptoms* of disease (Neuburger 1906: 196).

For Hippocrates and his followers symptoms were simply 'significant phenomena' (Heidel 1941: 62). Their consideration of symptoms as natural signs – those having the power to signify the same things in all times and places – was of the most comprehensive sort. A very early discussion of this type is found in Hippocrates' *Prognostic xxv*:

One must clearly realize about sure signs, and about symptoms generally, that in every year and in every land bad signs indicate something bad, and good signs something favourable, since the symptoms described above prove to have the same significance in Lybia, in Delos, and in Scythia. So one must clearly realize that in the same districts it is not strange that one should be right in the vast majority of instances, if one learns them well and knows how to estimate and appreciate them properly.

I have previously recalled an enduring example of his method, the detailed description of the famous *facies hippocratica* (Sebeok 1979: 6f.); another example may be cited from *Epidemics I* (Heidel 1941: 129):

The following were circumstances attending the diseases, from which I formed my judgments, learning from the common nature of all and the particular nature of the individual, from the disease, the patient, the regimen prescribed and the prescriber – for these make a diagnosis more favourable or less; from the constitution, both as a whole and with respect to the parts, of the weather and of each region; from the customs, mode of life, practices and age of each patient; from talk, manner, silence, thoughts, sleep or absence of sleep, the nature and time of dreams, pluckings, scratchings, tears; from the exacerbations, stools, urine, sputa, vomit, the antecedents of consequents of each member in the succession of diseases, and the abessions to a fatal issue or a crisis, sweat, rigor, chill, cough, sneezes, hiccoughs, breathing, belchings, flatulence, silent or noisy, hemorrhages, and hemorroids. From these things we must consider what their consequents also will be.

In *The Science of Medicine* Hippocrates also stated: 'What escapes our vision we must grasp by mental sight, and the physician, being unable to see the nature of the disease nor to be told of it, must have recourse to reasoning from the symptoms with which he is presented.' The means by which a diagnosis may be reached 'consist of observations on the quality of the voice, whether it be clear or hoarse, on respiratory rate, whether it be quickened or slowed, and on the constitution of the various fluids which flow from the orifices of the body, taking into account their smell and colour, as well as their thinness or viscosity. By weighing up the significance of these various signs it is possible to deduce of what disease they are the result, what has happened in the past and to prognosticate the future course of the malady' (Chadwick and Mann 1950: 87–9).

However, it was Galen, whose one and only idol was Hippocrates and whose medicine remained (on the whole) Hippocratic, who attempted to provide prognostics, wherever feasible, with a scientific underpinning, that is, to base his forecasts on actual observations. This he was able to do because he practised dissection and experiment: whereas Hippocrates studied disease as a naturalist, Galen 'dared to modify nature as a scientist' (Majno 1975: 396). 'Empirical method was first formulated in ancient medicine,' as systematic and detailed expression in the Hippocratic corpus (De Lacy 1941: 121), and became a part of the theory of signs for the Epicureans and Sceptics, in opposition to the Stoic rationalistic position. Philodemus' fragmentary treatise (c.40 B.C.) is by far the most complete discussion of a thoroughgoing methodological work uncovered (in the Herculaneum library) and extensively elucidated to date. Galen, despite all of his Platonic training, was later 'forced by his profession to be more empirical' (Phillips 1973: 174), even though this open-minded investigator, who continued to speak with the voice and authority of a scientist, did gradually turn into something of a dogmatic mystic (Sarton 1954: 59). He can therefore be regarded as a subtle founder of clinical semiotics as such (Neuburger 1906: 385). But he can also, very likely, be reckoned the first 'scientific' semiotician.

Galen's pen was as busy as his scalpel. In the course of his exceptionally bulky writings, he classified semiotics as one of the six principal branches of medicine, an ordering that had a special importance for its 'effect on the later history of medicine' (Phillips 1973: 172). The strength of Galenism, as Temkin (1973: 179) also emphasizes, 'reposed in no small measure in having provided medical categories ... for relating the individual to health and disease,' including 'semeiology (the science of signs).' Galen also divided the field into three enduring parts: in the present, he asserted, its concern was *inspection*, or diagnosis, in the past *cognition*, or anamnesis (etiology), and, in the future *providence*, or prognosis. His clinical procedure is depicted well by Sarton (1954: 6):

When a sick man came to consult him, Galen ... would first try to elicit his medical history and his manner of living; he would ask questions concerning the incidence of malaria and other ailments. Then the patient would be invited to tell the story of his new troubles, and the doctor would ask all the questions needed to elucidate them and would make the few examinations which were possible.

Galen regarded everything 'unnatural' occurring in the body as a symptom, and an aggregation of symptoms as a *syndrome*. He was fully aware that symptoms and syndromes directly reflected clinical observation, but the formulation of a diagnosis required causal thinking (Siegel 1973). He was the master of foretelling the course of diseases (Neuburger 1906: 383). Although his prognostications rested essentially and loyally upon the *Corpus Hippocratum*, his own anatomical knowledge and exactitude of mind predisposed him to build up his prognoses from a cogent diagnostic foundation.

Interpreting Symptoms

It would appear unreasonable to expect a finely attuned reciprocal conformation between internal states and 'reality,' between an *Innenwelt* and the surrounding *Umwelt*, or more narrowly between symptoms and their interpretations as an outcome over time or evolutionary adaption – *prodotto genetico*, in Prodi's (1981: 973) succinct formulation – that benefits an organism by raising its 'fittingness.' But such does not reflect the state of the art of diagnosis. The probabilistic character of symptoms has long been realized, among others, by the Port-Royal logicians (Sebeok 1976: 125). But their often vague, uncertain disposition was clearly articulated by Thomas Sydenham, the seventeenth-century physician often called the 'English Hippocrates' (Colby and McGuire 1981: 21). This much-admired doctor, held in such high regard by his brother of the profession, John Locke, was also known as the 'father of English medicine' (Latham 1848: xi). Sydenham was noted for his scrupulous recognition of the priority of direct observation. He demanded 'the sure and distinct perception of peculiar symptoms,' shrewdly emphasizing that these symptoms 'referred less to the disease than to the doctor.' He held that 'Nature, in the production of disease, is uniform and consistent; so much so, that for the same disease in different persons, the symptoms are for the most part the same; and the self-same phenomena that you would observe in the sickness of a Socrates you would observe in the sickness of a simpleton' (Latham 1848: 14). This assertion of his was, of course, quite mistaken, although the medical-student jape referred to by Colby and McGuire (1981: 23), 'that the trouble with psychiatry is that all psychiatric syndromes consist of the same signs and symptoms,' appears to be equally exaggerated. There are, to be sure, certain diagnostic difficulties inherent in the similarities between the symptomatology of functional syndromes and of those of the organic maladies. The marginal, or supplementary, symptoms of the former can, however, be assimilated according to specific criteria, such as are set forth, for instance, by Uexküll (1979).

This set of strictures leads me to a consideration of an aspect of symptom that is seldom mentioned in the literature, but that I have found both fascinating and, certainly for semiotics, of broad heuristic value. This has to do with *anomalies*, a problem that concerned, in a philosophical context, especially Peirce. According to Humphries (1968: 88), a naturally anomalous state of affairs is such 'with respect to a set of statements which are at present putatively true,' or, putting the matter in a more direct way, 'any fact or state of affairs which actually requires an explanation can be shown to be in need of explanation on the basis of existing knowledge' (1968: 89). The enigmatic character of semiotic anomalies can be especially well illustrated by clinical examples, where few existing models are capable of accounting for a multitude of facts. Medicine may, in truth, be one of the few disciplines lacking an overarching theory, although local, non-linear, and hence restricted and oversimple paradigms, such as the 'theory of infectious diseases,' certainly do exist.

Take as a first approach to the matter of anomalies the spirochaete *Treponema pallidum*. This virus, in its tertiary phase, may manifest itself as ('cause') aortitis in individual A, paretic neurosyphilis in individual B, or no disease at all in individual C. The latter, the patient with *asymptomatic* tertiary syphilis, can be said to have a disease without being ill. Note that a person may not only be diseased without being ill, but, conversely, be ill without having a specific identifiable disease. What can we say, in cases such as this, about the implicative nexus conjoining the 'proposition,' that is, the virus, with its consequent, expressed in some tangible manner or, on the contrary, mysteriously mantled? Are A, B, and C in complementary distribution, and, if so, according to what principle – the constitution of the patient, or some extrinsic factor (geographic, temporal, societal, age- or sex-related, and so forth), or a coalition of these? The influence of context, one suspects, may be paramount. This becomes overriding in the matter of hypertension – not a disease at all, but a *sign* of cardiovascular disorder

(Paine and Sherman 1970: 272) – which is realized in one and only one restricted frame: within that of patient/physician interaction, assuming the aid of certain accessories, such as a sphygmoscope. Semiosis is, as it were, called into existence solely under the circumstances mentioned; otherwise there are are no symptoms (the asymptomatic, i.e., so-called silent, hypertension lasts, on average, fifteen years) – there are no signs and there is, therefore, no determinate – that is, diagnosable – object.

Studies have shown that the majority of people who have gallstones go through life without palpable problems. The presence of these little pebbles of cholesterol that form in a sac that stores digestive juice can clearly be seen on X-rays: the shadows are the 'objective signs,' but most of them never cause pain, or any other symptom. They remain mute. They are, in other words, diagnosed only in the course of detailed check-ups, and thus require no surgical intervention.

Sensory experiences, at times, lead to semiosic paradoxes, such as the following classic contravention. A hole in one of my teeth, which feels mammoth when I poke my tongue into it, is a subjective symptom I may elect to complain about to my dentist. The dentist lets me inspect it in a mirror, and I am surprised by how trivially small the aperture – the objective sign – looks. The question is: which interpretation is 'true,' the one derived via the tactile modality or the one reported by the optical percept? The felt image and the shape I see do not match. The dentist is, of course, unconcerned with the size of the hole, filling the cavity he/she beholds.

It is a common enough experience that the symptom (for reasons ultimately having to do with the evolutionary design of the human central nervous system) refers to a different part of the body than where the damage is actually situated. 'The pain of coronary heart-disease, for example, is felt across the front of the chest, in the shoulders, arms and often in the neck and jaw. It is not felt where the heart is – slightly over the left' (Miller 1978: 22). Such a misreport is unbiological, in the sense that a lay reading could be fatal. An even more outlandish symptom is one for which the referent is housed nowhere at all, dramatically illustrated by a phantom limb after amputation. Miller (1978: 20) writes:

The phantom limb may seem to move – it may curl its toes, grip things, or feel its phantom nails sticking into its phantom palm. As time goes on, the phantom dwindles, but it does so in peculiar ways. The arm part may go, leaving a maddening piece of hand waggling invisibly from the edge of the real shoulder; the hand may enlarge itself to engulf the rest of the limb.

What is involved here is an instance of subjective – as against objective – pain, a distinction introduced by Friedrich J.K. Henle, the illustrious nineteenth-century German anatomist and physiologist, and generally perpetuated in classifications of pain ever since (e.g., Behan 1926). Subjective pain is described as having 'no physical cause for existence'; that is, there is no organic basis for its presence (indeed, with respect to a limb unhinged, not even an organ): it results 'of impressions stored up in the memory centers, which are recalled by the proper associations aroused' (Behan 1926: 74), which is to say that the pain remains connected with a framework of signification dependent upon retrospective cognizance. Referred pain and projection pain are closely allied; the latter is a term assigned to pain that is felt as being present either in a part that has no sensation (as in *locomotor ataxia*) or in a part that because of amputation no longer exists.

Certain symptoms – pain, nausea, hunger, thirst, and the like – are private experiences, housed in no identifiable site, but in an isolated annex that humans usually call 'the self.' Symptoms such as these tend to be signified by paraphonetic means, such as groans or verbal signs, which may or may not be coupled with gestures, ranging in intensity from frowns to writhings. An exceedingly knotty problem, which can barely be alluded to here, arises from several meanings of 'self' and how these relate to the matter of symptomatology. The biological definition hinges on the fact that the immune system does not respond overtly to its own self-antigens; there are specific markers that modulate the system generating antigen-specific and idiotype-specific cell lines – in brief, activate the process of self-tolerance. Beyond the immunological self, there is also a 'semiotic self,' which I have discussed elsewhere (Sebeok 1979: 263–7).

Another diacritic category of symptoms deserves at least passing mention. These a linguist might be tempted to dub 'minus features,' or symptoms of abstraction. Here belong all the varieties of *asemasia* (Sebeok 1976: 57, 1979: 58) – agnosia, agraphia, alexia, amnesia, amusia, aphasia, apraxia, etc., as well as 'shortcomings' like blurred vision, hardness of hearing, numbness – in short, symptoms that indicate a deficit from some ideal standard of 'normality.'

In any discussion of symptoms, it should be noted that even a syndrome or constellation of symptoms – say, of a gastronomical character (anorexia, indigestion, and haemorrhoids) – may not add up to any textbook case of disease labelling or terminology. Ensuing treatment may, accordingly, be denominated 'symptomatic,' accompanied by the supplementary advice that the patient remain under continuing observation. In some circumstances, 'the syndrome might be ascribed to psychologic etiology' (Cheraskin and Ringsdorf 1973: 37). What this appears to mean is that the interpretation of symptoms is often a matter involving, over time, a spectrum of sometimes barely perceptible gradations, entailing a progressively multiplying number of still other symptoms. It is also worth remarking that, temporally, or for predictive purposes, symptoms generally precede signs, which is to say that the orderly unfolding of evidence may be termed *prognostic.*

No one, at present, knows how afferent neuronal activity acquires meaning, beyond the strong suspicion that what is commonly called the 'external world,' including the objects and events postulated as being contained in it, is the brain's formal structure (logos). For all practical purposes, we are ignorant about how the central nervous system preserves any structure and assigns a meaning to it, how this process relates to perception in general, and how it induces a response. Implicit in this set of queries is a plainly linear model: for example, that fear or joy 'causes' increased heart rate. Not only does such a model seem to me far too simplistic, but there is not even a shred of evidence that it exists at all.

The future of symptomatology will clearly rest with program developments using computer techniques derived from studies of artificial intelligence. These are intended to mime and comple-

ment, if not to replace, human semiosic processes, such as judgment based on intuition (in one word, abduction). Such diagnostic
counsellors are already operational, as for example the program
termed *Caduceus* (McKean 1982). This program

examines a patient with fever, blood in the urine, bloody sputum from
the lungs, and jaundice. The program adds together numbers that show
how much each symptom is related to four possible diagnoses – cirrhosis
of the liver, hepatitis, pneumonia, and nephritis – and picks pneumonia
as top contender. The runner-up in score is hepatitis. But because
hepatitis has one symptom not shared with pneumonia (blood in the
urine), Caduceus chooses cirrhosis as first alternative. This process,
called partitioning, focuses the computer's attention on groups of related
diseases. (McKean 1982: 64)

The craft of interpreting symptoms has a significance far exceed-
ing the physician's day-to-day management of sickness. As Hippocrates had already anticipated, its success derives from its
psychological power, which critically depends on the practitioner's
ability to impress his/her skills on both the patient and their joint
environment (the audience gathered in his/her workshop, which
may consist of the patient's family and friends, as well as the physician's colleagues and staff). Dr Joseph Bell, of the Royal Infirmary
of Edinburgh, attained the knack with panache, leaving his
imprint on the detective story, following in the footsteps of Dr
Arthur Conan Doyle's fictional realization, Sherlock Holmes
(Sebeok 1981, Ginzburg 1983). According to recent medical thinking, the contemporary preoccupation with diagnosis – that is, doctor's perceived task, or pivotal drive, being to explain the meaning
of the patient's condition – rests in the final analysis with the doctor's self-assigned role as an authenticated expositor and explica-
tor of the values of contemporary society. Disease is thus elevated
to the status of a moral category, and the sorting of symptoms had
therefore best be viewed as a system of semiotic taxonomy – or, in
Russian semiotic parlance, a 'secondary modelling system.'

Lord Horder's dictum – 'that the most important thing in medicine is diagnosis, the second most important thing is diagnosis and

the third most important thing is diagnosis' (Lawrence 1982) –
must be true, because medical knowledge has risen to the status of
a means of social control. Symptomatology has turned out to be
that branch of semiotics that teaches us the ways in which doctors
function within their cultural milieu.

5

Indexical Signs

The poet Joseph Brodsky (1989: 44) has recently remarked that a study in genealogy 'normally is owing to either pride in one's ancestry or uncertainty about it.' Indeed, most contemporary workers in semiotics proudly trace their lineage, or try to, to Peirce, whom Max Fisch (1980: 7) once justly characterized as 'the most original and versatile intellect that the Americas have so far produced.' In this, he perhaps echoed Peirce's student and some-time collaborator in the early 1880s, Joseph Jastrow (1930: 135), who called his teacher 'one of the most exceptional minds that America has produced' and 'a mathematician of first rank.'

Of course, intimations of Western semiotics – sometimes under the distinctly indexical *nom de guerre* 'sem(e)iotic' – which, in a sense, culminated with Peirce, gradually sprouted out of the haze of millennia before him. And the 'doctrine' of signs, to which Peirce imparted so critical a spin, today clearly continues to flourish almost everywhere. His reflection (8:41) that 'human inquiries – human reasoning and observation – tend toward the settlement of disputes and ultimate agreement in definite conclusions which are independent of the particular standpoints from which the different inquirers may have set out' holds surely no less for semiotics than it applies in other domains of study and research.

In this chapter, I will look more closely at one of Peirce's greatest contributions to the study of semiosis – his notion of 'indexicality.' It should go without saying that this Peircean category, like every other, cannot be well understood piecemeal, without taking into account, at much the same time, the veritable cascade of other irreducible triadic relational structures which make up the armature of Peirce's semiotic – indeed, without coming to terms with his philosophy in its entirety. But this ideal procedure would be mandatory only were I bent on exegesis rather than engaged – taking Peirce's ideas as a kind of beacon – in a quest of my own. I should nonetheless give at least one example of the dilemma of selectivity by noting how Peirce tied together his notions of deduction and indexicality (2:96):

An Obsistent Argument, or *Deduction*, is an argument representing facts in the Premiss, such that when we come to represent them in a Diagram we find ourselves compelled to represent the fact stated in the Conclusion; so that the Conclusion is drawn to recognize that, quite independently of whether it be recognized or not, the facts stated in the premisses are such as could not be if the fact stated in the conclusion were not there; that is to say, the Conclusion is drawn in acknowledgement that the facts in the premisses constitute an Index of the fact which it is thus compelled to acknowledge.

Indexicality

It was Rulon Wells (1967: 104) who, in an article that even today amply rewards close study for its extraordinary fecundity, argued the following three interesting claims:

1. that Peirce's notion of the icon is as old as Plato's (i.e., that the sign *imitates* the signified);

2. that Peirce's notion of the symbol is original but fruitless;

3. that it is 'with his notion of index that Peirce is at once novel and fruitful.'

I will discuss some implications of the first of these statements in the next chapter. This is not the place to debate the second. The third assertion is – I enthusiastically concur with Wells – doubtless

true. Peirce's views on the index may in truth have been historically rooted in his interest in the realism of Scotus; '*hic and nunc*,'
he once observed, 'is the phrase perpetually in the mouth of Duns
Scotus' (1:458). 'The index,' he later amplified, 'has the being of
present experience' (4:447). Whatever the attested sources of his
ideas on this topic may have been, his innovativeness with respect
to the index is, as Wells (1967: 104) noted, due to the fact that
Peirce saw, as no one before him had done, 'that indication (pointing, ostension, deixis) is a mode of signification as indispensable as
it is irreducible.'

Peirce contended that no matter of fact can be stated without the use of some sign serving as an index, because *designators*
compose one of the main classes of indexes. He regarded designations as 'absolutely indispensable both to communication and to
thought. No assertion has any meaning unless there is some designation to show whether the universe of reality or what universe of
fiction is referred to' (8:368). Deictics of various sorts, including
tenses, constitute perhaps the most clear-cut examples of designations. Peirce identified universal and existential quantifiers with
selective pronouns, which he classified with designations as well
(2:289).

He called his other main class of indexes *reagents*. Since reagents
may be used to ascertain facts, little wonder they became the staple
of detective fiction, as was dazzlingly demonstrated in the famous
Sherlock and Mycroft Holmes duet in 'The Greek Interpreter' and
thereafter replayed by Conan Doyle's countless copycats.

Space permits but a single cited exemplification here of how this
detectival method of abduction (alias 'deduction') (see Eco and
Sebeok 1983) works in some detail. The *rei signum* of my choice
(Quintilian 8.6.22) involves, as it turns out, a bay mare, or yet
another horse, an animal which, for obscure reasons, has been
favoured in this context by dozens of novelists, from the 1747 episode of the king's horse in Voltaire's *Zadig*, to the chronicle of
Silver Blaze, John Straker's racehorse, to the many ensuing race-
horses of Dick Francis, and finally to Baskerville's incident of the
abbot's horse, by Eco. My parodic pick comes from Dorothy L.
Sayers's novel *Have His Carcase* (1932: 209–10).

In chapter 16 Harriet Vane hands over to Lord Peter Wimsey a shoe she has just found on the beach. He then proceeds to reconstruct – *ex alio aliud etiam intellegitur* (Quintilian 8.6.22) – a horse from this synecdoche:

He ran his fingers gently round the hoop of metal, clearing the sand away.

'It's a new shoe – and it hasn't been here very long. Perhaps a week, perhaps a little more. Belongs to a nice little cob, about fourteen hands. Pretty little animal, fairly well-bred, rather given to kicking her shoes off, pecks a little with the off-fore.'

'Holmes, this is wonderful! How do you do it?'

'Perfectly simple, my dear Watson. The shoe hasn't been worn thin by the 'ammer, 'ammer, 'ammer on the 'ard 'igh road, therefore, it's reasonably new. It's a little rusty from lying in the water, but hardly at all rubbed by sand and stones, and not at all corroded, which suggests that it hasn't been here long. The size of the shoe gives the size of the nag, and the shape suggests a nice little round, well-bred hoof. Though newish, the shoe isn't fire-new, and it is worn down a little on the inner front edge, which shows that the wearer was disposed to peck a little; while the way the nails are placed and clinched indicates that the smith wanted to make the shoe extra secure – which is why I said that a lost shoe was a fairly common accident with this particular gee. Still, we needn't blame him or her too much. With all these stones about, a slight trip or knock might easily wrench a shoe away.'

'Him or her. Can't you go on and tell the sex and colour while you're about it?'

'I am afraid even I have limitations, my dear Watson.'

...

'Well, that's quite a pretty piece of deduction.'

Peirce (2:289) pointed out that 'a scream for help is not only intended to force upon the mind the knowledge that help is wanted, but also to force the will to accord it.' As discussed in the previous chapter, perhaps Peirce's best-known example of a reagent – although a disconcerting one, for it seems exempt from his general rule that an index would lose its character as a sign if it had no interpretant (Ayer 1968: 153) – involved 'a piece of mould with a bullet-hole in it as a sign of a shot; for without a shot there would have been no hole; but there is a hole there, whether anybody has the sense to attribute it to a shot or not' (2:304). Here belong motor signs as well, as is commonly the case, they serve to indicate the state of mind of the utterer; however, if a gesture serves merely to call attention to its utterer, it is but a designation.

An index, as Peirce spelled out further, 'is a sign which refers to the Object it denotes by virtue of being really affected by that Object' (2:248) – where the word 'really' resonates to Scotus's doctrine of *realitas et realitas*, postulating a real world in which universals exist and general principles manifest themselves in the sort of cosmos that scientists try to decipher.

Peirce specified that, 'insofar as the Index is affected by the Object, it necessarily has some Quality in common with the Object, and it is in respect to these that it refers to the Object' (2:305). He further noted that it is a 'sign, or representation, which refers to its object not so much because of any similarity or analogy with it, nor because it is associated with general characters which that object happens to possess, as because it is in dynamical (including spatial) connection both with the individual object, on the one hand, and with the senses or memory of the person whom it serves as a sign, on the other hand.' Let it be recalled that all objects, on the one hand, and the memory, being a reservoir of interpretants, on the other hand, are also kinds of signs or systems of signs.

Thus indexicality hinges upon association by contiguity, a technical expression Peirce (3:419) understandably disliked, and not, as iconicity does, by likeness; nor does it rest, in the manner of a symbol, on 'intellectual operations.' Indexes, 'whose relation to their objects consists in a correspondence in fact ... direct the attention to their objects by blind compulsion' (1:558).

A grisly instance (only recently laid to rest) of association by contiguity was the right arm of the Mexican General Alvaro Obregón. Lost at the elbow during a battle in 1915, the limb had until the summer of 1989 been on display in a jar of formaldehyde at a large marble monument in Mexico City, where it acquired talismanic qualities referring to the ruthless former president. When the novelist Gabriel García Márquez suggested (Rohter 1989) that 'they should just replace [the decaying appendage] with another arm,' he was effectively advocating that the limb be transfigured from an index with a mystical aura into a symbol with historical significance.

Features of Indexicality

Iconicity and indexicality have often been polarized – although never by Peirce – with the same comparable labels in the most various fields, as if the two categories are antagonistic rather than complementary (Sebeok 1985: 77). So, for instance:

- James G. Frazer contrasted homeopathic with contagious magic, 'the magical sympathy which is supposed to exist between a man and any severed portion of his person';

- the Gestalt psychologist Max Wertheimer set apart a 'factor of similarity' from a 'factor of proximity';

- the neuropsychologist Alexander Luria distinguished similarity disorders from contiguity disorders in aphasic patients;

- linguists in the Saussurean tradition differentiated the paradigmatic from the syntagmatic axis, opposition from contrast, etc.

Contiguity is actualized in rhetoric, among other devices, by the trope of metonymy: the replacement of an entity by one of its indexes. The possessive relation between an entity and its index is often realized in grammar by the genitive case (Thom 1973: 95–8), as in Shakespeare's couplet 'Eye of newt, and toe of frog / Wool of bat, and tongue of dog' (*Macbeth*), with the preposition; and his line 'O tiger's heart wrapp'd in a woman's hide' (*King Henry vi*), without one. The *pars pro toto* proportion is also at the core of the anthropological and, in particular, psycho-sexual semiotic category known as 'fetish,' as will be discussed in chapter 6 (see also Sebeok 1989). In poetics, lyric verse has sometimes been professed to be imbued with iconicity; in contrast, epics are characterized as being imbued with indexicality.

The closely related notion of ostension, launched by Russell in 1948, and later developed by Quine, in the sense of ostensive definition, should be alluded to here at least in passing. The Czech theater semiotician Ivo Osolsobe (1979) has extensively analysed this concept in the somewhat different context of 'ostensive communication.' This is sometimes also called 'presentation' or 'showing.' Osolsobe wants to sharply distinguish ostension from idexicality, deixis, natural signs, communication by objects, and the like. However, I find his paradoxical assertion that 'ostension is the cognitive use of non-signs,' and his elaboration of a theory of ostension as a theory of non-signs, muddled and perplexing.

Temporal succession, relations of a cause to its effect or of an effect to its cause, or else some space/time vinculum between an index and its dynamic object, as Berkeley and Hume had already discovered but as Peirce went much farther to elaborate, lurk at the heart of indexicality. The epidemiologists, responsible for investigating the outbreak of a disease (i.e., an effect) impinging upon a large number of people in a given locality, seek for a source carrier (i.e., a causative agent), whom they call, in the root purport of their professional jargon, an 'index case,' who, and only who, had been exposed, say, to an unknown viral stockpile. It is in this sense that a Canadian airline steward, Gaetan Dugas, also known as the infamous 'Patient Zero,' was supposedly identified as *the* index case for AIDS infection in North America.

A given object can, depending on the circumstance in which it is displayed, momentarily function, to a degree, in the role of an icon, an index, or a symbol. Witness the Stars and Stripes:

- Iconicity comes to the fore when the interpreter's attention fastens upon the seven red horizontal stripes of the flag alternating with six white ones (together identical with the number of founding colonies), or the number of white stars clustered in a single blue canton (in all, identical to the number of actual states in the Union).

- In a cavalry charge, say, the flag was commonly employed to imperatively point, in an indexical fashion, to a target.

- The debates pursuant to the recent Supreme Court decision on the issue of flag burning present the Stars and Stripes as an emotionally surcharged problem, being a subspecies of symbol.

Peirce once stated uncommonly loosely that a sign 'is either an *icon*, an *index*, or a *symbol*' (2:304). But this plainly cannot be so. Once Peirce realized that the utility of his trichotomy was greatly enhanced when, in order to allow for the recognition of differences in degree, not signs but rather *aspects* of signs are being classified, he emended his statement thus: 'it would be difficult if not impossible, to instance an absolutely pure index, or to find any sign absolutely devoid of the indexical quality' (2:306), although he did allow demonstrative and relative pronouns to be 'nearly pure indices,' on the ground that they denote things but do not describe them (3:361). Ransdell (1986: 341) rightly emphasized that one and the same sign can – and, I would insist, must – 'function at once as an icon and symbol as well as an index'; in other words, that all signs necessarily partake of 'secondness,' although this aspect is prominently upgraded only in certain contexts.

Peirce, who fully recognized that an utterer and an interpreter of a sign need not be persons at all, would not in the least have been shocked to learn that semiosis, in the indexical relation of secondness – along with its elder and younger siblings, firstness and thirdness – appeared in terrestrial evolution about 3.6×10^9 years ago. Too, in human ontogenesis, secondness is a universal of infant pre-speech communicative behaviour (Trevarthen 1990). The reason for this is that the prime reciprocal implication between *ego*, a distinct sign maker, and *alter*, a distinguishable sign interpreter – neither of which, I repeat, need be an integrated organism – is innate in the very fabric of the emergent, inter-subjective, dialogic mind (Braten 1988).

Signs, inclusive of indexes, occur at their most primitive on the single-cell level, as physical or chemical entities, external or internal with respect to the embedding organism as a reference frame, which they may 'point' to, read, or microsemiotically parse – in brief, can issue functional instructions for in the manner of an index. Such an index, which may be as simple as a change in magnitude, a mere shape, a geometric change in surface area, or some singularity, can be significant to a cell because it evokes memories, that is, exposes previously masked stored information.

The following striking example, from the life of the ubiquitous prokaryotic bacterium *E. coli*, was provided by Berg (1976). This single-celled creature has multiple flagellae that it can rotate either clockwise or counter-clockwise. When its flagellae rotate clockwise, they fly apart, causing the organism to tumble. When they rotate counter-clockwise, they are drawn together into a bundle which acts as a propeller to produce smooth, directed swimming. Roaming about in the gut, the bacterium explores a chemical field for nutrients by alternating – its context serving as operator – between tumbling and directed swimming until it finds an optimally appropriate concentration of chemical attractant, such as sugar or an amino acid, for its replication. In doing so, it relies on a memory lasting approximately four seconds, allowing it to compare deictically, over short times and distances, where it *was* with where it is. On that basis, it 'decides,' with seeming intentionality, whether to tumble, stay in place, or swim and search for another indexical match somewhere else.

It may be pertinent to note that, with respect to their rhythmic movements, the *hic et nunc* that we humans perceive has a duration of three seconds. Poets and composers appear to be intuitively aware of this fact when they provide proper 'pauses' in their texts. Recent ethological work in societies the world over on ostensive and other body posture movements of an indexical character reveal that there are no cultural differences in the duration of these kinds of behaviours and that the time intervals last an average of 2 seconds for repeated gestures and 2.9 seconds for non-repeated gestures. According to the researchers, the 3 second 'time window' appears to be fully used up in these circumstances.

Manifestations of Indexicality

The brilliant neo-Kantian theoretical and experimental biologist Jakob von Uexküll (1864–1944), labouring in Hamburg in a very different scientific tradition and employing a discrepant but readily reconciliable technical jargon, was laying down the foundations of biosemiotics and setting forth the principles of phytosemiotics and zoosemiotics at roughly the same time as Peirce was elaborating general semiotics in the solitude of Milford. Unfortunately, neither knew of the other.

It fell to a contemporary German semiotician, Martin Krampen, in collaboration with Uexküll's elder son, Thure, to show in detail why and precisely how the Peircean distinctions apply to plants. Krampen (1981: 195–6) wrote in part:

If one wants to extend this trichotomy to plants on the one hand, versus animals and humans on the other, the absence of the function cycle [which, in animals, connects receptor organs via a nervous system to effector organs] would suggest that, in plants, indexicality certainly predominates over iconicity ... Indexicality, on the vegetative level, corresponds to the sensing and regulating, in a feedback cycle, of meaningful stimulation directly contiguous to the form of the plant.

After all, as Peirce once mused (3:205), 'even plants make their living ... by uttering signs.'

Indexical behaviour is found in abundance in animals too. As discussed in the previous chapter, the bird presciently named *Indicator indicator* by its ornithologist taxonomer is more commonly known as the 'black-throated honey-guide' in English. The honey-guide's singular habit of beckoning and pointing various large mammals, including humans, towards nests of wild bees was first noted in southwest Mozambique in 1569. When the bird discovers a hive, it may seek out a human partner, whom it then pilots to the hive by means of an elaborate audiovisual display.

The display proceeds roughly in the following manner. The normally inconspicuous honey-guide calls out, emitting a continuous sequence of chirring notes. Then it flies, in stages, to the nearest tree, lingering motionless on an easily seen branch until the pursuit recommences. When embarking on a flight – which may last from two to twenty minutes and extend from 20 to 750 metres – the bird soars with an initial downward dip, its white tail feathers saliently outspread. Its agitated ostensive comportment continues until the vicinity of the objective, a bees' nest, is reached. Avian escorts and their human followers are also capable of reversing their roles in this indexical *pas de deux*: people can summon a honey-guide by mimicking the sound of a tree being felled, thereby triggering the behaviour sequence described.

Such words as *symptom, cue, clue, track, trail,* and so forth, are among the high number of English quasi-synonyms of *index.* I return once again to Peirce's telling example of secondness – that footprint Robinson Crusoe found in the sand, 'and which has been stamped in the granite of fame,' and which 'was an Index to him that some creature was on his island' (4:531). This illustrates a key attribute of indexicality, to wit: the operation of *renvoi,* or referral, which directs Robinson Crusoe back to some day, presuably prior to Friday, in the past. The index, as it were, inverts causality. In Friday's case, the vector of the index points to a bygone day in that a *signans,* the imprint of some foot in the sand, temporally rebounds to a *signatum,* the highly probable presence of some other creature on the island. Thom (1980) has analysed some fascinating ramifications of parallels, or the lack of them, between semiotic transfers of this sort and physical causality and the genesis of symbols – the footprint which, Peirce noted, at the same time 'as a Symbol, called up the idea of a man.'

The historian Carlo Ginzburg (1983) has exposed commonalities among art historians who study features of paintings by means of the so-called 'Morelli method,' medical diagnosticians and psychoanalysts bent on eliciting symptoms, and detectives in pursuit of clues. Ginzburg invokes a canonical trio of physicians – Dr Morelli, Dr Freud, and Dr Conan Doyle – to make out a very convincing case for their and their colleagues' parallel dependence on indexical signs. He shows that their historical provenance, features, symptoms, clues, and the like, are all based on the same ancient semiotic paradigm: the medical. (As discussed in the previous chapter, that model was of course implicit in the Hippocratic writings and made explicit by Galen.)

Indexes included for Peirce 'all natural signs and physical symptoms ... a pointing finger being the type of the class' (3:361). The 'signs which become such by virtue of being really connected with their objects' comprehended for him 'the letters attached to parts of a diagram' as much as 'a symptom of disease' (8:119). Writing to Lady Welby, he contrasted 'the occurrence of a symptom of a disease ... a legisign, a general type of a definite character,' to its 'occurrence in a particular case [which is] a sinsign' (8:335).

Ginzburg (1983: 88–9) has adroitly traced back the origins of the medical model based upon the decipherment and interpretation of clues, clinical and otherwise, to two coupled sources: (1) early hunting practices, as proto-humans retrogressed from the effects, an animal's tracks and other leavings – prints in soft ground, snapped twigs, droppings, snagged hairs or feathers, smells, puddles, threads of saliva – to their actual cause, a yet unseen quarry; and (2) Mesopotamian divinatory techniques, progressing magically from an actual present cause to a prognosticated future effect – animals' innards, drops of oil in water, stars, involuntary movements.

Ginzburg's subtle arguments, which make learned use of the overarching medieval and modern comparison between the world – metaphorically, the Book of Nature – and the book, both assumed to lie open ready to be read once one knows how to interpret indexical signs, draw comprehensively upon Old World sources. But he could as easily have cited nineteenth-century American fiction, such as James Fenimore Cooper's Leatherstocking saga, to other mythic accounts of 'Noble Savages,' to illustrate dependence on sequences of indexical cues, available to immediate perception, which enabled the art of pathfinding through the wilderness landscape. Thus alone, Uncas, the last of the Mohicans, is able to read a language, namely, the Book of Nature, 'that would prove too much for the wisest' of white men, Hawkeye; so also Uncas's crucial discovery of a footprint, in one Cooper's novels, makes it possible for Hawkeye to confidently assert, 'I can now read the whole of it' (Sebeok 1990).

So also Robert Baden-Powell, in his military manual *Reconnaissance and Scouting* (1884), adapted Sherlock Holmes's technique of 'deduction,' that is, inferring important conclusions from seemingly insignificant clues, when teaching his young troopers how to interpret enemy locations and intentions by studying indexical topographical signs, including footprints.

For the farmer, forester, and professional gardener, it is essential, if only for reasons of economy, to be able to sort out animal tracks (Bang and Dahlstrom 1972). We know from contemporary field naturalists' accounts that nature continually provides a record of the previous night's activities printed in the ground for anyone who cares to follow them. Thus Tinbergen (Ennion and Tinbergen 1967) used to spend many an hour in countryside detection, reading the stories written in footprint code, revelling in the patterns of light and shade in the stillness of the morning.

The body of any vertebrate, including humans, is composed of a veritable armamentarium of more or less palpable indexical markers of unique selfhood. Certain mantic practices like haruspication from patterns of liver flukes and palmistry but also some highly consequential pseudo-sciences – graphology today (Furnham 1988), phrenology in the past – hinge pivotally on secondness; according to Kevles's (1985:6) awesome account, the chief of the London Phrenological Institution told Francis Galton, himself to become no mean biometrician, that people of his head type – his skull measured twenty-two inches around – 'possessed a sanguine temperament, with considerable self-will, self-regard, and no small share of obstinacy' and that 'there is much enduring power in such a mind as this – much that qualifies a man for roughing it in colonising.'

Some forms of entertainment, such as stage conjury and circus animal acts, rely crucially on the manipulation of indexical signs. So do certain crafts, such as handwriting authentication and, of course, identification, criminal or otherwise, by fingerprinting (Moenssens 1971) – mentioned no less than seven times by Sherlock Holmes – according to a phenotypic system devised by Galton in the 1890s. In 1894 Mark Twain's fictional character Pudd'nhead Wilson became the first lawyer in the world to use fingerprints in a criminal case, antedating Scotland Yard by eight years. Such indexes are called in the business 'professional signs.' Erving Goffman (1963: 56), the distinguished sociologist, called them 'positive marks' or 'identity pegs.' Preziosi (1989: 94–5) further connects the methods of Morelli, Voltaire's Zadig, Sherlock Holmes, and Freud with Hyppolyte Taine's *petits faits*, or his system of cultural and artistic indexes, and with Peirce.

All such devices likewise richly hinge on secondness, as was already evident in proto-semiotic works like Alphonse Bertillon's *Service de signalements* (1888) and *Instructions signalétiques* (1893). He dubbed his system of measurements of the body 'anthropometry.' On the genotypic plane, so-called 'DNA fingerprinting' can, arguably, identify with a discrimination far beyond anything available in forensics heretofore – in fact, with absolute certainty, if properly used – every individual, excepting an identical twin, even by a single hair root on a small piece of film displaying his or her unique sequence of indexical DNA molecules.

The Study of Indexicality

Natural sciences in general work empirically by decoding indexes and then interpreting them. The crystallographer Alan Mackay (1984) in particular has shown how his field shares with divination 'a belief that nature can be made to speak to us in some metalanguage about itself, a feeling that nature is written in a kind of code,' and how augurers decode nature's indexical messages by magic, scientists by logic. Crystallographers are strongly and consciously influenced by techniques of decryption, and they have heavily borrowed from the semiotic vocabulary of the cryptographers: for example, they speak of X-ray diffraction photographs as message texts.

The distinctive pheromonal function of human chemical signatures (Toller and Dodd 1989), nowadays studied under the newly designated scientific rubric of 'semiochemistry,' has in fact been compared with individual fingerprints. Patrick Süsskind based his beautifully researched novel *Das Perfum* entirely on the indexical facets of human semiochemistry and its devastating repercussions.

The field encompasses the study of odours, of which Peirce (1:313) wrote in an amazingly lyrical, yet seldom remembered, passage that these 'are signs in more than one way' which 'have a remarkable tendency to presentmentate themselves ... namely, by contiguous association, in which odors are particularly apt to act as signs.' He continued in this personal vein:

A lady's favorite perfume seems to me somehow to agree with that of her spiritual being. If she uses none at all her nature will lack perfume. If she wears violet she herself will have the same delicate finesse. Of the only two I have known to use rose, one was an artistic old virgin, a *grand dame*; the other a noisy young matron and very ignorant; but they were strangely alike. As for those who use heliotrope, frangipanni, etc., I know them as well as I desire to know them, Surely there must be some subtle resemblance between the odor and the impression I get of this or that woman's nature.

Our immune system utilizes approximately as large a number of cells dispersed throughout our body as the number of cells that composes a human brain. These endosymbiotic – or, as I would prefer, endo*semiotic* – aggregations of spirochetal remnants, functioning – as the Nobel laureate Niels Jerne (1985) has shown – in the open-ended manner of a finely tuned generative grammar, constitute an extremely sensitive, sophisticated repertory of indexical signs, circumscribing, under normal conditions, our unique biological selfhood. Sadly, secondness can go awry under pathological conditions, when, for instance, one is afflicted with certain types of carcinoma or an auto-immune disease, or ultimately even when administered immuno-suppressors after an organ transplant.

Most of the huge literature on indexicality has been played out either in the verbal arena or else in the visual (Sonesson 1989: 38– 65). Peirce was right as usual in arguing for the predominance of indexicality over iconicity, with respect to the mode of production, in photographs: 'they belong to the second class of signs, those by physical connection' (2:281). This has now been documented in Phillippe Dubois's outstanding study, *L'Acte photographique* (1988). And it has long been obvious that metonymy – especially the indexical method of *pars pro toto* – far outweighs the uses of metaphor in films.

In the verbal domain, indexicality has chiefly preoccupied, although with rather differing emphases, philosophers of language and professional linguists. Bar-Hillel's (1970) conspectus is useful in this regard. Bar-Hillel knew, of course, that it was Peirce who had launched the terms 'indexical sign' and 'index.' He goes on to remind his readers that Russell used instead 'ego-centric particulars,' though without resolving whether Russell rediscovered indexicality independently of Peirce or simply relabelled it. He further recalls that Nelson Goodman coined 'indicator' and Reichenbach 'token-reflexive word.'

The overall interest of linguists and philosophers in indexical expressions is bound up, as I understand it, with their search for an ideal language, consisting of a set of context-free sentences, to use as an instrument for probing the universe *sub specie aeternitatis*. In Ayer's (1968: 167) phrasing, the argument has been about 'whether language can be totally freed from dependence upon context.' Ayer was unable to decide this for himself, and I believe that the matter is still wide open. However, whether or not this indecision has any serious consequences for indexicality in general or for Peirce's view of this matter in particular seems to me quite doubtful. For as Ayer (1968: 167) thought as well, 'although a reference to context within the language may not be necessary for the purposes of communication, there will still be occasions, in practice, when we shall need to rely upon the clues which are provided by the actual circumstances in which the communications are produced.'

Peirce once insisted that an index was quite essential to speech (4:58). So what do linguists mean by an index? For many, this term simply and broadly refers to membership-identifying characteristics of a group, such as regional, social, or occupational markers; for others, more narrowly, to such physiological, psychological, or social features of speech or writing that reveal personal characteristics as the voice quality or handwriting in a producing source. Indexicals of these sorts, sometimes called expressive features, have been analysed for many languages and in a wide range of theoretical contributions.

In addition, there is a vast, separate literature, not as a rule sub-sumed by linguists under indexicality, devoted to different types of deixis. By this linguists refer to a whole range of commonly gram-maticalized roles in everyday language behaviour, that is, to the ways in which interlocutors anchor what they talk about to the spa-tio-temporal context of their utterance. Person deixis, social deixis, place deixis, time deixis, and discourse deixis are the major types distinguished in the literature (Levelt 1989: 44–58). Karl Bühler (1934: 107) called the relevant context of the utterance *Zeigfeld*, or indexical field, and the anchoring point of this *hic et nunc* field its *Origo*, or origin (see also Jarvella and Klein 1982).

Deictics can vary considerably from language to language and can often be – as, for example, in Wolof (Wills 1990) – very knotty in structure. One examination of the typological and universal characteristics of personal pronouns in general, over a sample of seventy-one natural languages, claimed the existence of systems ranging from four to fifteen persons (Ingram 1978). In this array, the English five-person system seems highly atypical, and if this were true, it could lead to fundamental questions about Peirce's and other philosophers' seemingly natural 'I-It-Thou' tripartition.

Only a native speaker of Hungarian can appreciate, if not always articulate, the richly differentiated set of terms of address which speakers must control to produce utterances appropriate to vari-ous roles and other contextual variables. For instance, to simplify, but not much: two academics of the same sex and approximate rank and age are unable to converse at ease in Hungarian without knowing each other's exact date of birth, because seniority, even if by one day, strictly determines the terms of address to be used in that dialogue (see also Lyons 1977).

Otto Jespersen (1922) casually coined the term 'shifter' to refer to grammatical units which cannot be defined without a reference to the message. In 1957 Jakobson reassigned shifters to the Peircean syncretic category of indexical symbols, which are, in fact, complex syncategorematic terms, where code and message inter-sect (1971: 132).

In a remarkable study of a single four-word sentence consisting of a modal auxiliary, a person-deictic pronoun, a verb, and the verb's complement, Fillmore (1973) has hinted at the incredible intricacy demanded of a linguistic theory if it is to adequately capture the conceptual richness of even the simplest sentences. Such a theory must incorporate principles for deriving at least the complete syntactic, semantic, and pragmatic description of a sentence, a theory of speech acts, a theory of discourse, and a theory of natural logic. Although all of these are foci of a considerable amount of research activity today, I know of no overarching theory which meets all of these demanding conditions.

Barwise and Perry (1983: 32–9) coined the expression 'efficiency of language' for locutions – even though these retain the same linguistic meaning – which different speakers use in different space-time locations and with different anchoring in their surroundings, and which are susceptible to different interpretations. To put it another way, the productivity of language depends decisively on indexicality, which is therefore 'extremely important to the information-carrying capacity of language.' These authors convincingly argue that philosophical engrossment with context freedom, that is, with mathematics and the eternal nature of its sentences, 'was a critical blunder, for efficiency lies at the very heart of meaning.' However this may be, linguists at present have no inkling of, let alone a comprehensive theory for, how this commonplace, global human enterprise is carried out.

Perhaps the most one can do is to follow Jacob von Uexküll's suggestion (see Thure von Uexküll 1989) that reality reveals itself in *Umwelten*, or those parts of the environment that each organism selects with its species-specific sense organs, each according to its biological needs. Everything in this phenomenal world, or self-world, is labelled with the subject's perceptual cues and effector cues, which operate via a feedback loop that Uexküll called the functional cycle. Nature (the world, the universe, the cosmos, true reality, etc.) discloses itself through sign processes, or semioses. These are of three distinct types:

- semioses of information, emanating from the inanimate environment;

- semioses of symptomatization, where the source is alive (this is equivalent to George Herbert Mead's 'unintelligent gestures');

- semioses of communication (Mead's 'intelligent gestures').

The first and second form indispensable, complementary steps in each biosemiosis. The observer reconstructs the exterior sign processes of the observed from the perceived stream of indexes, but never their interior structures, which necessarily remain private. The transmutation of such sign processes into verbal signs are meta-interpretations which constitute objective connecting structures that remain outside the subjective world of the observed living entity; these are 'involved in its sign processes only as an inducing agency for its perceptual sign and as a connecting link to its operational sign' (Uexküll 1989: 151).

How reference – the index-driven circuit between the semiosphere (Lotman 1984) and the biosphere – is managed by sign-users and sign-interpreters remains, despite the best efforts of Peirce and of his many followers, a profound enigma. Theories of mapping and modelling have not progressed beyond disciplined speculation. Notwithstanding that, I remain intuitively attracted to Wheeler's (1988) closed loop of the world viewed as a self-synthesizing system of existences. His teacher, Niels Bohr, considered, rightly in my opinion, such questions as how concepts are related to reality as ultimately sterile. Bohr once replied to this very question: 'We are suspended in language in such a way that we cannot say what is up and what is down. The word *reality* is also a word, a word which we must learn to use correctly' (French and Kennedy 1985: 302).

6

Iconic Signs

While indexicality clearly constitutes a fundamental form of sign-ing, next in line is iconicity, the second of Peirce's three basic cate-gories. In many ways, iconicity is a much more fundamental form of semiosis than is indexicality. In this chapter I will look at the essential features, and at the multifarious manifestations, of this phenomenon.

Iconicity

As Wells (1967) has judiciously pointed out, Peirce's 'notion of icon is as old as Plato's (the sign *imitates* the signified).' It was indeed Plato who bequeathed the concept of mimesis (Lausberg 1960: 554) to theoreticians of literature from Aristotle to Wimsatt (1954), who was responsible for consciously restoring the term *icon* into the critical vocabulary at mid-century by using it as the key word in the title of one of his important collections of essays. How-ever, the icon acquired its entirely novel perspective in conse-quence of Peirce's juxtaposition in the very particular context of his second trichotomy of signs – the one he called his 'most funda-mental' (2:275) division, and the one which has certainly become his most influential – first with the index, and then both of the former pair with the symbol. The icon and the index embody sign-relations which are in the natural mode – respectively of likeness and of existential connection – as against the symbol, which is in the conventional mode, or reflective of a relation that is characterized by 'an imputed quality,' to cite Peirce's matchless precision of expression (1:588).

Peirce's icon can scarcely be understood when wrenched out of the total context of his semiotic. And yet iconicity has generated a plethoric literature. Why has iconicity – and its complementary obverse *aniconism* (the religious prohibition of images) – become the focus of so much passionate concern on the part of many? Wallis (1975: 157), among others, has alluded to the suggestive power of iconic signs, and the implications of this puissance for the history of culture. The magic efficacy of the kind of icon called *effigy* has long been recognized in ritual experience, whether in a sermon by Donne, when he proclaimed, in 1661, that 'in those that are damned before, we are damned in Effigie,' or, in an appropriate relic display of puppets in front of a fraternity house on virtually any American campus in season, in a ceremony to secure victory for one's football team. The ritual system of certain cultures is constructed of iconic signs: thus, among the Rotinese, a major premise of rituals is based on the equation of humans and plants, and defined by icons cast in a life-enhancing botanic idiom (Fox 1975: 113).

What does it mean to say that an iconic sign is based on 'similarity,' which Peirce introduced on occasion into his *definiens*? This was criticized by Eco (1976: 192–200) as a naïve conception, because icons are culturally coded, that is, conventionally so 'in a more flexible sense.' Of course, we know that Peirce had himself held exactly this view when he asserted that any material image 'is largely conventional in its mode of representation,' although 'it may be called a *hypoicon*' (2:276), and when he singled out 'icons in which the likeness is aided by conventional rules' (2:279). However this may be, the usefulness of similarity, particularly in its classical juxtaposition with contiguity, as pointed out several times in previous chapters, derives from the pervasiveness of the pair in many fields of intellectual endeavour throughout Western history. Thus, while I welcome Eco's imaginative and searching analysis, I still favour retaining the terminology that troubles him: 'similarity,' and the rest, constitute, in my view, a time-honoured set of primes whose usefulness in a wide range of human sciences has been amply proven, but whose pertinence to semiotic discourse becomes fully manifest only if properly applied. The notion of an icon is very much impoverished when viewed, as it so often is, in isolation rather than in the total context of a fully rounded science of signs.

The Incidence of Iconicity

There are numberless instances of iconicity in zoosemiotic discourse, involving virtually all known channels – that is, forms of physical energy propagation – available to animals for message transmission. Bateson (in Sebeok 1968: 614–28) has even tried to explain why genotypic controls have often evolved to determine iconic signalling, and has brilliantly argued that an understanding of human dreaming 'should throw light both on how iconic communication operates among animals and on the mysterious evolutionary step from the iconic to the verbal.' The same startling thought, of the evolutionary immediacy of dreaming in humans that allows for a degree of consciousness during periods of sleep and hence a certain discontinuity of the subject/object distinction inherent in iconic coding, seems to have occurred independently to Thom (1975: 72f.).

Just a few illustrations of the use of iconic signs in the animal world will suffice here. The iconic function of a chemical sign may be accurately measured by fluctuations in the intensity of insect odour trails laid by successful foragers, for example, in various species of ants. The actual quantity of the emitted pheromone depends directly on the amount and quality of the source of nourishment: 'as a food supply and the odor intensity of the trail to it diminish, fewer foragers are attracted' (Butler 1970: 45); that is, the pheromone acts as an iconic sign vehicle inasmuch as it relates in analog fashion to the waxing or waning of the guiding odour spots (although a crawling insect may use supplementary channels – redundantly or according to strict rules of code-switching – such as sight, touch, sun-compass reaction, and orientation by polarized light from a blue sky, but always, under such conditions, in an iconic fashion). Genetically programmed iconicity plays a pivotal role in deception involving smell and taste, colour and shape, sound, and, of course, behaviour, as graphically described by Hinton (1973). Sometimes an animal even alters its surroundings to fit its own image by fabricating a number of dummy copies of itself to misdirect predators away from its body, the live model, to one of several replicas it constructs for that very purpose. And this is only one among a number of iconic antipredation devices contrived by different species of a highly interesting genus of spiders known as orb-weavers (Wickler 1968: 56f, Hinton 1973: 125f.). The theory of mimicry, which finds many applications throughout both plants and animals, as Wickler (1968) has shown, deals with a range of natural phenomena involving the origin of all species and all adaptations. However, associations consisting of models and their mimics constitute but one special set of biological events connecting signs with things signified by 'a mere relation of reason' (Peirce 1:372), in which case the sign is an icon, so that the former must be integrated, *in toto*, with the far more general and deep theory of iconicity.

I cannot resist recounting one particularly elegant (if sometimes disputed) example of a complex piece of invertebrate behaviour that evolved, as it were, to function as an iconic sign in the visual or tactile mode. Unravelled by Kloft (1959), it has to do with a certain ant-associated aphid species. These small, soft-bodied insects, very vulnerable to predator attack, are protected and tended by ants with which they communicate by an alarm pheromone that functions to stabilize their association. Their relationship is further reinforced by the fact that the ants 'milk' the aphids by vibrating their antennae against an aphid's back; the aphids then secrete droplets of honeydew which are consumed by the ants. Kloft realized that this congenial relationship rests on a 'misunderstanding' and proposed, as a working hypothesis, that the hind end of an aphid's abdomen, and the kicking of its hind legs, constitute, for an ant worker, a compound sign vehicle, signifying, from its perspective, the head of another ant together with its antennal movement. In other words, the ant, in an act of perversion of the normal trophallaxis occurring between sisters, identifies the replica (the rear end of the aphid) with the model (the front end of the ant) and solicits on the basis of this misinformation, treating a set of vital biological releasers out of context, that is, in the manner of an effigy. The multiple resemblances between model and replica are so striking, subtle, and precisely effective that they can hardly be explained away as an evolutionary coincidence (Wilson 1975: 422).

Features of Iconicity

I have already cited in previous chapters Peirce's rough division of icons into images, diagrams, and metaphors (2:227), and mentioned his seeming lack of interest in the third. Icons are still too often simplistically identified with mere images, such equations giving rise to shallow and unenlightening theories, especially of art. The neglect of diagrams is particularly incomprehensible in view of the fact that they loomed large in Peirce's own semiotic research, and that they have been reviewed by at least three careful scholars, at some length (Zeman 1964, Roberts 1973, Thibaud 1975).

Peirce (2:282) has explicitly spelled out that 'many diagrams resemble their objects not at all in looks; it is only in respect to the relations of their parts that their likeness consists.' Elsewhere, he stressed that 'a diagram has got to be either auditory or visual, the parts being separated in one case in time, in the other in space' (3:418). There follows a crucial passage (3:419), which all linguists should read through to the end. Peirce established there, among other things, that 'language is but a kind of algebra,' or method of forming a diagram. He then continues: 'The meanings of words ordinarily depend upon our tendencies to weld together qualities and our aptitudes to see resemblances, or, to use the received phrase, upon associations by *similarity*; while experience is bound together, and only recognizable, by forces acting upon us, or, to use an even worse chosen technical term, by means of associations of *contiguity*.' He dwells upon (7:467) 'the living influence upon us of a *diagram*, or *icon*, with whose several parts are connected in thought an equal number of feelings or ideas ... But the icon is not always clearly apprehended. We may not know at all what it is; or we may have learned it by observation of nature.' To put it tersely, I am of the opinion that no critique of iconicity that ignores Peirce's existential graphs in their multifarious implications can be taken seriously or regarded as at all viable.

A surprisingly prevalent solecism assumes that icons, that is, images, are necessarily confined to the visual modality. Sometimes a semantic constriction of this sort is imposed by deliberate choice. 'There is substantial agreement,' according to one outstanding experimenter searching for the locus of short-term visual storage, also called iconic memory, 'that the terms icon, visual image, and persistence of sensation may be used interchangeably' (Sakitt 1975: 1319). But a moment's reflection about the iconic components of spoken natural language should suffice to check this counter-productive terminological limitation. We ought also to be mindful, in this connection, of the many multi-sensory iconic representations that pervade human and other animal existence in everyday life. One such sphere which is permeated by iconicity is, broadly speaking, that of small-group ecology, illustrated, for instance, by seating behaviour (Lott and Sommer 1967) as one kind of spatial positioning: at a family gathering, we expect to find the 'head' of the household at the 'head' of the table, etc. As studies of various alloprimates have likewise clearly shown, 'the relative position and distance of the various members of a group from one another reflect the nature of the social relations between them' (Hall and DeVore 1965: 70). Moreover, Kummer (1971: 233) has insightfully reviewed the essentially iconic connection of social relations and spatial arrangements in animals in general, plausibly concluding with the suggestion that 'territorial tendencies ... can reemerge in the handling of information.' In other words, there exists a diagrammatic correspondence between the *signans*, the spatial arrangement, and the *signatum*, the social organization, in a fashion analogous to the isomorphic relation between a geographical area and any map that purports to represent it.

Contemplation of the icon sooner or later tends to turn from legitimately semiotic concerns, in the technical sense, to intractable, indeed mind-boggling, philosophical problems of identity, analogy, resemblance, and contrast (Ayer 1968: 151), similarity and dissimilarity, arbitrariness and motivation, geometry and topology, nature and culture, space and time, life and death. The experience is like entering a fun house furnished with specular reflections and distorting mirrors, doubles and replicas, emphatic stimuli and superoptimal models, and being taken for a ride in the clair-obscure on one of Gombrich's (1951) pedigreed hobby-horses. Eco (1976: 212), with his customary stylish wit, has provided his readers with some guideposts through this jungle of equivocations, not ignoring the final, possibly fatal, ambiguity that 'everything resembles everything else.' To answer his animadversions upon the icon, recall my example in the third chapter vis-à-vis the issue of regression (the representation of *La Gioconda*).

The essential features of iconicity can be summarized as follows (see also Bouissac et al. 1986):

- The notion of icon, and allied concepts, have come under con-tinuous and, at certain periods, quite intense discussion through-out the centuries linking Plato and Peirce. The tendency of ideas to consort with one another because of similarity became a pow-erful principle for explaining many mental operations, and thus an important chapter in the history of ideas, where the story was, as it still is, retold with infinite variations.

- Peirce's (1:313, 383, 502) 'resemblance-association,' out of which his icon must have crystallized, derives its startling novelty from being embedded in a progressively more complex, profound, and productive semiotic matrix, which is, moreover, conceived as both a theory of communication and a theory of signification. Although Peirce's classification of signs has become the one con-stant lodestar in debates about iconicity since 1867, the level of discussion is substantially diminished when the icon is, as is often done, quarantined from the total context of his unique brand of the 'doctrine' of signs, or when the intricacies of his semiotic are insufficiently grasped (having perhaps been culled from second-ary sources, or worse).

- There are no pure iconic signs; in fact, 'no actual sign is an icon' (Ayer 1968: 140). The transformation of deiconization is frequent; the reverse process of iconization more seldom encountered. It is plausible to assume that there may be a diachronic tendency toward an equilibrium in mixed systems of signs (such as gesture-languages used in some deaf communities).

- Iconicity plays a decisive role in shaping everyday life in all cultures. Iconic signs suffuse humanity's communication codes, verbal no less than non-verbal.

- Iconic signs are found throughout the phylogenetic series, in all modalities as circumscribed by the sense organs by which members of a given species are able to inform themselves about their environment. Signal forgery (i.e., the phenomenon of mimicry), in fact, all deceptive manoeuvring by plants, animals, as well as humans, often crucially depends on iconicity.

- Unsolved riddles concerning this pervasive mode of producing, storing, and transmitting iconic sign tokens abound. Some of these pertain to logic, some to psycho-physiology, others to ethology. Their solution awaits the advent of new analytical tools, the most promising among which by far – for it shows how the process of copying operates throughout the molecular level, governs perception, imbues the communicative systems of animals as well as of humans, and constitutes a fundamental principle of sociobiology, in brief, is capable of integrating globally far-reaching problems of a universal character involving mutual dynamic relations between signifier and signified (Thom 1974: 245) – are likely to come from catastrophe theory (e.g., Stewart 1975), which will render them susceptible to topological analysis.

The Study of Iconicity

Around the turn of the last century, labouring entirely outside the grand philosophical currents that culminated in Peirce's semiotic, his contemporary, Ferdinand de Saussure, contributed to the progress of the field with much more modest restraint, both departing from a strictly linguistic base and making constant reference back to linguistic standards, but wholly with a view to the future. Although Saussure never used the term, he did provide, as a passing example of an iconic sign, the scales of justice (Saussure 1967 [1916]) representing the equilibrium between sin and punishment. The actual provenance of his ideas about the typology of signs remains a tantalizing mystery. He appeared to have evinced no special interest in iconicity, and although his Franco-Swiss successor, Bally (1939), did so to a limited extent, our common fund of knowledge about the theory of signs and symbols has not been materially enhanced in the Saussurean tradition. Yet the breakthrough in the field did ultimately originate in France, to wit, in Thom's (1973) brilliant foray into this aspect of semiotics. It should surprise no one that Peirce's ideas, particularly about the icon, should have found so sympathetic an echo in the work of this distinguished creator of topological models, for Peirce expected his existential graphs to also explicitly contribute toward an understanding of topological laws (4:428f.); indeed, his 'system is topological throughout' (Gardner 1968: 56).

Thom (1975: 72f.) assumes that the principal role of the central nervous system of animals is to map out localized regions to simulate the position of the organism in its environment, as well as to represent objects, such as prey and predator, that are biologically and/or socially crucial with respect to its survival or well-being. That is to say, an animal is constantly informed and impelled by meaning-bearing sign vehicles designed to release pertinent motor reflexes (irms), such as approach (say, toward a prey) or withdrawal (say, from a predator), or surrogate verbal responses in the human, as in a transitive subject-verb-object sentence, a syntactic pattern which can be viewed as a temporal transcription of a biological event in space-time, predation, as its archetypal paradigm. Among animal behaviourists, Schneirla (1965: 2) has argued persuasively, in support of his biphasic theory, that 'operations which appropriately increase or decrease distance between organisms and stimulus sources must have been crucial for the survival of all animal types' in the evolution of behaviour. Thom (1975: 73) has extended this line of reasoning to humans, who, he says, by the act of naming have replaced iconic representations of space-time interactions with symbols.

The genesis of icons was sketched, all too briefly, by Thom (1973). In countless instances, images appear naturally, but copies of this sort are ordinarily devoid of semiotic value – a person's shadow cast upon the ground, a shape reflected in water, a foot imprinted in sand. Such everyday spatial images are necessarily endowed with certain physical, geometric properties, but they attain semiotic status only under special circumstances. For a shadow to be cast, as in the first example, the model must be illuminated by a luminous source, the light hitting the body, thus defining its shadow. In the second example, a specular image is similarly formed in the reflecting surface. In neither example is the resulting image permanent: it is bound to vanish with the disappearance of the model (or luminous source). However, the third example illustrates a new phenomenon that Thom calls 'plasticity' of the receptor system. The footprint does not necessarily decay when the foot is withdrawn (or the sun goes under): the formative stimulus alters the equilibrium of the receptor system when impressing the shape of the model; here the image becomes a memory trace (Sakitt 1975). Thom designates the dynamic state involved in such a transaction 'competence,' implying the possibility of irreversible temporal interaction. A modification in the first example underlines the distinction: should a person's shadow be cast upon a photographic plate instead of the unsensitized ground, that person's image may forever be fixed owing to the competence of the receptor system. Using the concepts suggested, one can envisage the formation of images equistable with their models, or more so, as termite mound constructions faithfully display in, so to speak, 'frozen,' or fossilized, products the social behaviour of these great insect architects, becoming available for a study of their behavioural evolution long after the extinction of the colony itself (Emerson 1938).

At this stage it can be claimed that life has been attained. A living being L fabricates, at some temporal remove, another living being L′, isomorphic with L. L′ will soon supplant L. Thom claims that his feature of plasticity activates the genetic code, giving rise to a self-replicating, mutable molecular system that is also environment-sensitive. The process involved is foreshadowed by the kind of inorganic local explosion that occurs in photographic emulsification. It becomes particularly plain in embryological development, which may be among the most dramatic forms of iconization: it is nature's design for unfolding the growth and differentiation of a structure isomorphic with the parent by virtue of a spatial-temporal translating operation. On the molecular level, this same mechanism is realized when the DNA double helix is replicated to generate two helices, each containing one old strand and one newly made one.

At the other end of the ontogenetic ladder of life, Thom invites us to consider the phenomenon of perception: this can be regarded as a modification of dynamic competence by the sensory impact of external reality, very much as Socrates had instructed Theaetetus. Any competent system, for example, the mechanical and hydrodynamic components of cochlear partition and the acoustic cortex, or the retina and the visual cortex, etc., rapidly recovers its percipient virginity, indispensable for total and permanent competence, while its plastic faculty guarantees that the sense impressions remain stored in the memory.

In Thom's panoramic conspectus, the formation of icons appears throughout the entire scale of nature as a manifestation of a universal dynamic of irreversible character: a model ramifies into a replica isomorphic with it. Frequently, however, this process employs a reversible interaction, due to the perennial oscillation of the thermodynamics between a Hamiltonian conservative viewpoint (expressed in the First Law) and the Heraclitean viewpoint, 'time's arrow' (expressed in the Second Law). In all interactions between the two indispensable moieties of the sign, the relation of signified to signifier must obey this universal flux: the signified engenders the signifier in an eternal process of branching. But the signifier re-engenders the signified each time that we interpret the sign. In biological terms, this is to say that the descendant as signifier can become the parent as signified, given the lapse of one generation.

Thom has vastly more to say, albeit in brief compass, about the image which bears on deiconization, stylization, decomposition, aging, and death, drawing a far-reaching distinction between the physical capacity of an icon to resist the noise factor inherent in any communicative exchange, and its biological capacity to evoke other forms biologically or sociologically important or 'interesting.'

Seeking common cause with Peirce, Thom probes the heart of signification. The transcendent feature of both is a soaring imagination. Their shared scientific instrument for the invention and discovery of new truths, as well as their device for reordering old ones, is a branch of mathematics capable of dealing with discontinuous and divergent phenomena, a special part of the theory of singularities. These two figures of charismatic depth bracket a century of more or less pedestrian divagations about the sign, as well as occasionally inspired extensions and applications of semiotic notions over most parts of the verbal and nonverbal domains.

The genetic code, the metabolic code (hormone-mediated intercellular transactions), the nonverbal communicative codes used in a very high number of organisms including humans, our unique verbal code and its differentiated participation in all manner of artistic functions, whether literary, musical, pictorial, architectural, choreographic, theatrical, filmic, or of diverse hybrid formations, and finally, comparisons among any of the aforementioned – these all continue to be on the agenda of contemporary semiotic science. Peirce and Thom cast a biunique spell that enthrals us, and it would be instructive to inquire sometime into the source of this fascination. The catastrophe theory developed by Thom in the 1960s was aimed first at embryology, where it could, in principle, account for each point of bifurcation as the development of a cell diverges from that of its immediate neighbours. Later, Thom extended his theory to evolution in general, reproduction, thinking, and, last but not least, the generation and transmission of verbal and nonverbal signs. It so happens that images are a major feature of his theory; he has proved that, despite the almost limitless number of discontinuous phenomena that can exist, there are only a certain number of different images that actually occur. He called these 'elementary catastrophes,' and has shown that, in a space having no more than four dimensions (such as our 'real' world), there are exactly seven such transformations.

7

Fetish Signs

As everyone can ascertain from the *Oxford English Dictionary*, the English vocable *fetish* was directly adopted from the Portuguese substantive *feitiço*, 'charm, sorcery' (Spanish *hechizo*; both from the Latin *facticius*, 'factitious,' meaning 'artificial, skilfully contrived'). Originally, the term was applied to any of the objects used by the people of the Guinea coast and neighbouring regions as talismans, amulets, or other means of enchantment, 'or regarded by them with superstitious dread.' Portuguese sailors allegedly minted the appellation in the fifteenth century when they observed the veneration that West Coast Africans had for such objects, which they wore on their person (see also Herskovits 1947: 368). The earliest English citation, as further reported in the *OED*, dates from a 1613 work by Purchas, *Pilgrimage* (6.15.651): 'Hereon were set many strawen Rings called *fatissos or Gods*.'

Writers on anthropology, following Brosses (1760), began using *fetish* in the wider sense of an inanimate object being worshipped by 'savages' on account of its supposed inherent magical powers, or as its animation by a spirit. More generally still, *fetish* referred to something irrationally reverenced. In 1869 McLennan, who framed totemism as a theoretical topic, also invented the notorious formula: totemism is fetishism plus exogamy and matrilineal descent (but see Lévi-Strauss 1962: 18). Van Wing then wrote (1938: 131) an oft-cited amplification about the fetish as a metaphor/metonym opposition.

The purpose of this chapter is to look at fetish as an example of semiosis that overlaps several sign categories. Although fetishism is common among mammals, it is a particularly good example of the fecundity of human semiosis involving the body, the mind, and culture simultaneously.

The Origin of Fetishism as 'Deviation'

One fruitful way of classifying religions has been to ask in the case of each: where is the divine (the object of religious responses) primarily sought and located, and what sort of response is primarily made to it? According to this principle of division, religions may be partitioned into three major groups: sacramental, prophetic, and mystical. Details of this were spelled out by Alston (1967b), following a suggestion by William James; but Auguste Comte and Charles de Brosses specifically interpreted the fetish as a basis for their theories concerning the origin of religion.

The divine in the sacramental religion is said to be chiefly sought in things, which are thought of as capable of capturing natural forces – inanimate things, such as pieces of wood, relics of saints, statues, crosses; or food and drink, such as bread and wine or baptismal water; or living things, such as the totemic animal of the group, the sacred cow, the sacred tree; or processes, such as the movements of the sacred dance. In very primitive forms of sacramental religion, when the object itself, perhaps possessing animate existence in and of itself, is responded to as divine, that object has, in early anthropological practice, been designated a fetish. Such a fetish could be wrought to have positive effects – such as to heal or cure sickness – and even used to induce erotic disposition, that is, to affect and alter 'natural' social relations.

Clearly, it was the assignment of the latter capability that led to the eventual espousal of the term in clinical, and thence in legal, discourse to describe the enhancement of sexual activity in the presence of a type of object which is, for others, not at all, or if so but weakly, endowed with a compulsively sexual (paraphiliac) connotation. Gebhard (1969: 72) quite properly envisions 'the whole matter of fetishism as a graduated phenomenon. At one end of the range is slight preference; next is strong preference; next is the point where the fetish item is a necessity to sexual activity; and at the terminal end of the range the fetish item substitutes for a living sexual partner.' Indeed, as will become clear, sorting by degree is the only procedure that makes sense when the matter is viewed from the semiotic standpoint.

The notion of 'fetishism of the commodities' (Erckenbrecht 1976) has become one of the cardinal concepts and slogans of the Marxist heritage as applied to the analysis of the relationship between people and products, or between use-value and exchange-value. Geras (1971: 71) sees the origins of this concept in the more fundamental distinction between 'essence' (i.e., 'real' social relations) and 'appearance' (the outer manifestation of such relations). He writes 'It is because there exists at the interior of capitalist society, a kind of internal rupture between the social relations which obtain and the manner in which they are experienced, that the scientist of the society is confronted with the necessity of constructing reality against appearances. Thus this necessity can no longer be regarded as an arbitrary importation into Marx's own theoretical equipment or something he merely extracted from other pre-existing sciences ... [It is] seen to lead, by a short route, to the heart of the notion of fetishism.'

In short, to invest a commodity with powers which are not present or inherent is to elevate it to the status of a fetish; it is in this way that money, or capital in general, comes to be 'fetishized.' Jhally (1987: 29) – whose concern is with fetishism in television and magazine advertising – recently reformulated this process in quasi-semiotic parlance when commenting that 'fetishism consists of seeing the meaning of things as an inherent part of their physical existence when in fact that meaning is created by their integration into a system of meaning.' Earlier, Baudrillard (1981: 92) made a similar point when he noted that it is the sanctification of the system as such, 'the commodity as system,' that reinforces 'the fetishist fascination.'

The Fetish in Psychology and Sexology

Psychopathia sexualis (1886), by the forensic psychiatrist Richard von Krafft-Ebing, contained the first systematic collection of data relating to 'pathological' fetishism. This text, with its view of sex as perverted and disgusting, came to exert a great, baleful, and seemingly perpetual influence. He wrote extensively of sex crimes and sexual variations or deviations, which he considered based upon genetic defects.

As far as I have been able to trace, it was Krafft-Ebing who first referred to the notion of the fetish as a 'perversion,' that is, something that required shame and social sanctions to control it. According to his descriptions, a fetish was a non-human object – a part of the body or something contiguous to it, such as clothing – which served as an impetus to sexual arousal and orgasm. The Teutonic doctor, in fact, considered all acts other than marital coitus for the purpose of procreation, and all surrogates for penile/vaginal intercourse – for example, voyeurism, exhibitionism, transvestitism, sadomasochism – as 'perversions' to be reprehended.

Krafft-Ebing's 'method' is illustrated by his report of a case (no. 101) of hair-fetishism, which I cite from Kunzle (1982: 53), who – after the French police doctor Paul Garnier's monograph (1896: 70) – uses it to illustrate 'the degree of moral vindictiveness' evinced by the authorities and approved of by Krafft-Ebing. According to this retold story, a seventeen-year-old boy was watching a show in the Tuileries gardens, while pressing up to a girl 'whose hair he silently, amorously rolled between his fingers, so softly that she did not even notice. Suddenly two plainclothes policemen sprang upon him. One seized with his hand the boy's erect penis through his trousers, and cried "*At last we got you ... after all the time we've been watching you!*"' The boy was then sentenced to three months in jail.

A standard comprehensive textbook of psychiatry by Freedman, Kaplan, and Sadock (1972) likewise defines the use of fetishes (in an explicitly sexual context) in metonymic terms: 'The process of achieving sexual excitement and gratification by substituting an inanimate object such as a shoe, piece of underwear, or other article of clothing for a human love object.' This definition is substantially repeated under the rubric of 'Other Sexual Deviations' [*sic*], where only 'a foot or a lock of hair' is added to the enumeration of common sexual fetishes. (A recent conspicuous instance of foot fetishism is displayed in Martin Scorsese's short film *Life Lessons*; this is realized by his camera's – or the painter's – obsessive dwelling over Rosanna Arquette's feet.) In point of fact, it is very common in psychiatric literature to find references to the attraction a patient may have for an inanimate object as 'inordinate' or 'pathological.'

A recent exchange (6 March 1987) from 'The Kinsey Report,' a syndicated newspaper column by my colleague June Reinisch, epitomizes the current scientific view of the subject:

Q. – I am a male in my mid-20s. Since age 9, I have been strongly attracted to women's feet, shoes and stockings. I become sexually aroused thinking about foot odor and sometimes have erections in public places from fantasizing about this. I feel extremely guilty and think most people would think I'm perverted. Do you think I'm sick? Do I need professional help? Why am I this way?

A. – I think that you should consult a psychotherapist who is experienced in working with sexual problems. He or she can help you determine exactly what role these desires play in your life, and then the two of you can decide what type of therapy (if any) is necessary for you to form long-lasting, close relationships. Fetishism is a behavior in which sexual arousal depends on an inanimate object, a certain body part or the like – in short, on something other than the whole person. This area has not been fully examined scientifically. Very little is known about the causes of fetishistic behavior, except that it is thought to originate early during psychosocial development. Scientists also don't know how many people have sexual fetishes but it is clear that this behavior is much more common in men than in women. A variety of body parts, items of clothing and odors have been mentioned in reports of individual fetishism.

It is clear first of all that both parties in the exchange view the reported fetishistic comportment as constituting a sexual 'problem,' possibly even a 'perverted' form of behaviour, or one at least likely to require psychotherapeutic intervention. This is so in spite of Reinisch's concession that very little is known about the causation or ontogeny of the kind of behaviour described.

Reinisch also echoes an opinion common among clinicians – that fetishism is much more common in men than in women. This presumption was held by Freud (1927; see Vigener 1989) as well as by Kinsey (1953: 679) and his collaborators who considered fetishism to be an 'almost exclusively male phenomenon.' Freud and his epigones even held that fetishism is *the* male perversion *par excellence.* Schor (1985: 303) put it in a nutshell: 'female fetishism is in the rhetoric of psychoanalysis, an oxymoron.'

For Schor's subject, George Sand, the female fetish happens to be a wound; but wounds, Schor (1985: 304) asserts, 'are not generally fetishized by men' – a questionable claim. Fetishistic attraction to cripples – or more broadly to 'discredited' individuals who bear stigmata in Goffman's sense (1963), as also to one-legged females, and even crutch fetishism (Schindler 1953) – abounds in the literature. For instance Morris (1969: 170) reports the following case: a young boy 'was leaning out of a window when his first ejaculation occurred. As it happened, he saw a figure moving past in the road outside, walking on crutches. When he was married he could only make love to his wife if she wore crutches in bed.'

Reinisch implicitly subscribes to the view of the fetish as an essentially indexical sign – especially a synecdochical sign ('something other than than the whole person') – although, of course, her idiom is other than semiotic. Indeed the fetish is, as here, commonly regarded as a fixation on the *pars pro toto.*

The most extensive recent study of the fetish in sexology is to be found in John Money's *Lovemaps* (1986). He once more offers a conventional definition: 'an object or charm endowed with magical or supernatural power; an object or part of the body charged, for a particular person, with special sexuoerotic power' (1986: 261). In his lemma on 'fetishism,' however, there is a hint of a wider view (to which I shall return) when Money (1986: 265) points out that there 'is no technical term for the reciprocal paraphiliac condition in which the fetish, for example, a uniform, must belong to the self.'

Mainly, what we find in Money's book is a routine catalogue of some objects that have been pinpointed by numerous clinicians as typical fetishes. Pornographers fabricate and sell objects – including pictorial and written displays – arranged according to similar categories, designed to cater to every conceivable fetishistic taste.

Money classifies (1986: 65f.) tangible objects – or, technically, imagery – in addition to those appealing to the eye, as either haptic or olfactory, available in immediate perception or in fantasy. The former pertain to feelings of pressure, rubbing, or touch, which may be generated internally (as by an enema or other inserted arte-fact) or externally (by the application of fabrics, fur, hair, etc.). A tactual token may also be a live creature, wriggling and/or furry; thus, in one reported case, a woman habitually placed a dog in her crotch, 'as an adjunct to masturbation and orgasm,' but she later substituted a small infant in the same position (1986: 64).

Leather (e.g., shoes) and rubber or plastic (e.g., training pants) fetishes bridge the gap between touch and smell, as did James Joyce's fetish for soiled knickers (Wilson 1989). Olfactory fetishes characteristically carry the smell of some portion of the human body, especially of those garments that cover sexual parts (fecal or urinary odour, odour of sweat, menstrual odour, smell of lacta-tion). These garments are sometimes also sucked or chewed.

Although Money does not emphasize this, the use of fetishes by females seems considerably more prevalent than has been explic-itly recognized in the literature thus far. Freud's judgment was obviously dictated by his theoretical preoccupation with the castra-tion complex, according to which fixation or regression to prior psycho-sexual stages of development underlies deviations, so that castration anxiety is the central component of fetishism.

Kinsey's traditional supporting opinion may have been due to nothing more that a prejudicial sampling error. For instance, com-pulsive stealing of objects which are of no intrinsic value to the thief but which have obsessive semiotic significance – treated in sexology under the heading of 'kleptophilia' – seemingly does occur in women more often than in men, but the connection is not always explicitly recognized (see Zavitzianos 1971, relating female fetishism to exhibitionism and kleptomania).

Moreover, reports like the following are not uncommon: 'A young girl experienced her first orgasm when clutching a piece of black velvet as she masturbated. As an adult, velvet became essential to her sexually. Her whole house was decorated with it and she only married in order to obtain more money to buy more velvet' (Morris 1969: 169). Similarly, the fixation of Imelda Marcos on her 500 bras and 2,700 pairs of shoes appears to be a well-publicized case of something more than run-of-the-mill female fetishism.

Children of both sexes frequently cling to an object – à la Linus and his celebrated blanket. Such an object may be related by contiguity to a parent or to the infant's early material surroundings. According to some psychiatrists (Freedman et al. 1972: 637), this 'is a security operation that should be distinguished from fetishism in which the normal sexual object is substituted by another.' It is further asserted in this source that fetishism of this latter type 'is not known to occur in childhood.' However, this judgment may be due to psychiatrists' clinging to the prejudice that a fetish, in order to be defined as such, must produce genital sexual satisfaction (usually deemed 'deviant' as well), and that the use of objects to produce a fetishistic effect necessarily occurs relatively late in adolescence. Nevertheless, transitory objects present in the child's immediate environment earlier on may, eventually, be promoted to the status of a full fetish, and so this again seems to be only a matter of degree (Sperling 1963, Roiphe 1973, Bemporad et al. 1976).

In passing, a syndrome sometimes called 'Pygmalionism,' which refers to a fetish in the shape of a female statue or life-sized rubber doll, should be mentioned here. From a semiotic viewpoint, such an object would constitute an index strongly tinged with iconicity. (To a lesser degree, the rarer cases of tattoo fetishism, as reported by Weimann 1962, may involve iconic indexes, too.)

Still other fetishes – as for instance diamond engagement rings, gold wedding bands, and class rings or pins exchanged as tokens of going steady by teenagers (Money 1986: 63) – can be taken as indexes overlaid, in an erotic frame of reference, with a pervasive symbolic significance that is widely understood within a culture. Money itself, or, more broadly, property, is commonly reported to turn into capitalistic fetish objects (Becker and Schorsch 1975 and Stratton 1987).

The Fetish in Semiotics

I turn now to a fuller consideration of the fetish as a semiotic problem. As can be gleaned even from the discussion thus far, it is clear that a fetish is

- a sign, namely, that it is

- a predominantly indexical sign; and that, moreover, it is

- an indexical sign of the metonymic species, usually a *pars pro toto* synecdoche; and that

- this indexical sign is, as a rule, intermingled with both iconic and symbolic elements in various proportions, depending on the context of its use.

With respect to the last point, an important consequence of the semiotic model of the fetish is that it is not necessary for the represented object to be fully present to the organism before information about it can influence internal semiosis ('thought') and induce what Peirce (7:372) called 'gratific' action.

In another terminology, a fetish could be regarded as a model (*aliquid*), but such that this simulacrum is often more potent than the object (*aliquo*) that it stands for (*stat pro*). Its reference (*renvoi*) is, as it were, reminiscent in efficacy to that of a caricature to the subject that it represents. This accords with Morris's (1969: 209) view that the art of caricature is entirely concerned with the process of stimulus extremism. Features exaggerated in caricatures are, as a rule, supernormal equivalents of normal juvenile features or of sexual parts, such as female breasts and buttocks.

As we have seen, the term 'fetish' has hitherto been principally employed in the fields of anthropology and psychiatry (including especially psychoanalysis) and, in a narrower, more focused sense –

yet quite extensively – in studies of erotic and sexual behaviour in humans. The notion of 'fetish' has to do, in all these conceptions, with an obsessive maintenance of self-image.

To my knowledge, thus far only Christian Metz (1985) has reflected on the 'fetish' in chiefly semiotic terms, but even he has done so only in a strictly circumscribed technical environment, namely, in relation to photography. Metz feels that because of two features – relatively small size and the possibility of a look that may linger – a photograph, as opposed to the cinematic lexis, is better fit, or more likely, to work as a fetish, that is to say, as something that signifies both loss (Freudian 'symbolic castration,' which is metaphoric) and protection against loss (which is metonymic). However, let me here set aside the matter of the photograph-as-fetish, which Metz then ingeniously relates to death (or the fear of death) and conversation (embodied as looking, glancing, gazing). Instead, I would prefer briefly to review and ponder the implications of the more relevant ethological problem variously dealt with under such headings as the 'supernormal signal/stimulus' or the 'superoptimal sign.'

The point I want to make about such signs was neatly captured by Oscar Wilde's celebrated aphorism (from *A Woman of No Importance*, act 3), 'Nothing succeeds likes excess,' itself anticipated by Shakespeare's lines 'To gild refined gold, to paint the lily, / To throw perfume on the violet ... / Is wasteful and ridiculous excess' (*King John*, 4.2.11f.).

In short, a sign is deemed 'supernormal' when it surpasses a 'normal' sign in its effectiveness as a releaser (meaning, the discharge of appropriate behaviour). According to Guthrie's (1976: 19) excellent account of the anatomy of social organs and behaviour, so-called supernormal signs 'occur in the form of extra-large social organs, i.e., increasing signal strength by increasing signal amplitude.' Thus, in certain species of animals, antlers and horns are used as an estimation of rank; they therefore either 'grow to gigantic size among the older males, or develop specialized modifications, like filling in between the tines to form palms, thereby increasing the visual effect from a distance.'

In particular, anal and genital organs – or just those about which mankind habours so many taboos – tend to become modified into semiotic organs for several reasons: in part, because mammals, having, in general, a well-developed smelling apparatus, tend to use faeces and urine as part of their signing behaviour ('who was where and when?'); and, in part, because of the sexual overtones of different mammalian ways of urination. Genitalia have frequently acquired heavy semiotic import and have become ritualized into a set of signs conveying oppositions such as maleness/femaleness or aggression/submission, while having also been elaborated into specialized social ornamentation that is residually related to their ancestral copulatory role.

The phenomenon of the supernormal stimulus object has been demonstrated many times in studies of animal behaviour, especially in one exemplary piece of work by Tinbergen and Perdeck (1950). In brief, these two investigators (among other interesting achievements) found that they could devise a supernormal stimulus object consisting of an artificial model in which some sign aspects are exaggerated relative to the natural object. Such a supernormal stimulus was provided by a long red knitting needle with three white rings near the tip. In the event, this was more effective than a naturalistic head and bill of an adult gull in evoking a pecking response from herring-gull chicks.

It should also be noted that, in experiments such as this one, the strength of the response to the stimulus situation varies from context to context, including that of the internal state of the responding animals. In the famous experiment designed to identify the stimulus characters important for the male three-spined stickleback, the maximal effectiveness of the red belly display depends on the stage of the respondent's breeding cycle and whether he is on his territory.

Writing about domestic cats, the ethologist Leyhausen (1967) observed that 'substitute objects' can become supernormal objects, as when a sated cat disports itself with a ball of paper in an intensive catching game, while perfectly 'adequate' prey mice run around under its very nose. Indeed, fetishistic attachments are commonplace among vertebrates – particularly in mammals, as well as in many birds.

I would argue that a fetish is just a supernormal sign, a 'misplaced response' (Lorenz 1971: 160), if you will, standing for – and indeed amplifying by a process of ritualization – some natural object, upon which an individual has become preferentially imprinted in lieu of the object itself. (For a more likely mechanism, see Leyhausen 1967.) But this definition requires a considerable expansion of the concepts of fetish and of fetishism to encompass erotic aestheticism in general, as well as positive attachments which can only by interpretative extension, if even then, be considered erotic (e.g., saints' relics or a rabbit's-foot charm).

Such attachments normally occur between a child and its mother, and again when the child grows up and falls in love with another human being. Attachment to an exclusive love-object or sexual partner, eventuating in a relationship which animal behaviourists call pair-bonding, involves in fact a live fetish: the love-object is a *pars pro toto* in the sense that, say, the female mate comes to stand for all marriageable females. 'The strongly sexual aesthetic responses to specific "beautiful features" of the male and female body demand particular attention,' for these are elicited by characters 'which are immediate indicators of hormonal sex functions' (Lorenz 1971: 159). Lorenz goes on to give many examples from art and from fashion of the production of such 'super-optimal dummies,' pinpointing those characters which are exaggerated for this purpose; other instances are listed and discussed by Morris (1969).

In this perspective, what in the literature of the erotic and the sexological is called a fetishistic attachment may be viewed as a form of mal-imprinting. As Morris (1969: 169) writes: 'Most of us develop a primary pair-bond with a member of the opposite sex, rather than with fur gloves or leather boots ... but the fetishist, firmly imprinted with his unusual sexual object, tends to remain silent on the subject of his strange attachment ... The fetishist ... becomes isolated by his own, highly specialized form of sexual imprinting.'

8

Language Signs

The mutual relationship between semiotics and linguistics is to be conceived of as either coordinate or hierarchical. If the relationship is hierarchical, there are two possiblities: either linguistics is superordinate, that is, it subsumes semiotics; or semiotics is superordinate, that is, it subsumes linguistics. Each of these three conjunctions has been variously put forward, but only the third has enjoyed sustained support. The first two can thus be disposed of briefly.

The view that semiotics and linguistics are coequal is maintained on utilitarian rather than abstract grounds. As Metz (1974: 60), for instance, has expostulated, 'In theory, linguistics is only a branch of semiotics, but in fact semiotics was created from linguistics ... For the most part semiotics remains to be done, whereas linguistics is already well advanced. Nevertheless there is a slight reversal. The post-Saussurians ... have taken the semiotics he foresaw and are squarely making it into a translinguistic discipline. And this is very good, for the older brother must help the younger, and not the other way around.' Unfortunately, Metz's argument is riddled with fallacies, the most serious among them being the historical one: semiotics was not at all created from linguistics, but, most likely, out of medicine as has been discussed throughout the previous chapters, and also had far deeper roots in the annals of humanity. Sometimes, however, the fraternal metaphor enjoys adminstrative sanction; thus Rice University, in 1982, created a Department of Linguistics and Semiotics (Copeland 1984: x).

Roland Barthes (1967: 11) may have been unique in his advocacy of the radical stand that semiology (alias semiotics) is but 'a part of linguistics: to be precise, it is that part covering the *great signifying unities* of discourse. By this inversion [of Saussure's celebrated dictum, more of which below], we may expect to bring to light the unity of the research at present being done in anthropology, sociology, psychoanalysis and stylistics round the concept of signification.' Of this passage, one, of Barthes's memorialists remarked: 'Even if language were the only evidence semiologists had, this would not make semiology part of linguisitics any more than the historians' reliance on written documents makes history a part of linguistics. But semiologists cannot rely on language alone; they cannot assume that everything named is significant and everything unnamed insignificant' (Culler 1983: 73–4). Prieto's opinion (1975: 133) – 'malgré l'attrait que peut exercer ce point de vue [i.e., Barthes's], je considére qu'il est insoutenable' – is shared by most semioticians and others. So, in this chapter, I will look at how semioticians and linguists view verbal and non-verbal semiosis.

The Study of the Verbal Sign

The subject matter of semiotics is often said to be 'the communication of any messages whatever' (Jakobson 1974: 32) or 'the exchange of any messages whatever and of the system of signs which underlie them' (Sebeok 1985: 1). Its concerns include considerations of how messages are, successively, generated, encoded, transmitted, decoded, and interpreted, and how this entire transaction (semiosis) is worked upon the context. Further questions revolve around problems of coding, phylogenesis and history, ontogenesis, loss of semiosic capacity ('asemasia'; see Sebeok 1979: 71), and the like. A message is equivalent to a string of signs. And signs, as we have seen throughout this book, are classifiable according to many (often partially overlapping) criteria: common oppositions may comprehend subjective signs, or symptoms, versus objective signs; 'wanted' signs, or signals, versus 'unwanted' signs, or noise; signs versus symbols (Maritain 1943, Cassirer 1944: 31,

Alston 1967a); icons versus indexes, and both against symbols; and so forth. The distinction which is most immediately pertinent here, however, is the one between nonverbal signs (the unmarked category) versus verbal signs (the marked category). This differentiation – which places semiotics in a superordinate position over both linguistics and the putative discipline, with, as yet, no universally agreed upon global designation, which studies nonverbal signs – enjoys a most respectable tradition among both philosophers and linguists.

The early development of the notion 'verbal sign' out of its Stoic beginnings has been expertly tracked by Telegdi (1976: 267–305), but for the continuation of the story since the seventeenth century we must begin anew with Locke. In the two-page concluding chapter of his *Essay* (1690: 720–1), where he dealt with the division of the sciences, Locke abruptly introduced the term *semiotics* (with a minor variation in spelling), briefly defining it as the 'Doctrine of Signs,' and explaining that its business 'is to consider the Nature of Signs, the Mind makes use of for the understanding of Things, or conveying its Knowledge to others.' A bit further in the same paragraph, Locke goes on to observe: 'to communicate our Thoughts to one another, as well as record them for our own use, Signs of our *Ideas* are also necessary. Those which men have found most convenient, and therefore generally make use of, are articulate Sounds. The Consideration then of *Ideas* and *Words*, as the great Instruments of Knowledge, makes no despicable part of their Contemplation, who would take a view of humane Knowledge in the whole Extent of it.' Locke's epistemological classification here is based, as Armstrong (1965: 380) rightly points out, 'upon the special theory of relations between *thing, idea,* and *word.*' And, as Deely (1985: 309–10) says, these key terms, 'words and ideas,' are here used by Locke synecdochically; that is, by the former Locke means verbal signs, in the ordinary sense of any and all units of language, whereas he equates the latter with objects (1690: 47). At any rate, in these short passages, Locke does establish two points: first, that 'words,' or the verbal, constitute but one class of signs; but that, second, for humans, this class is a priviliged one.

The Alsatian philosopher Lambert, who was strongly influenced by Locke, published his workmanlike *Semiotik* (1764) some three-quarters of a century later, devoting the first of its ten chapters to types of signs other than verbal, while the rest of his monograph dealt with language.

The importance Peirce attached to his doctrine of signs is vividly illustrated by a famous quotation from a letter he wrote to Lady Welby, on 23 December 1908: 'Know that from the day when at the age of 12 or 13 I took up, in my elder brother's room, a copy of Whately's *Logic* and asked him what Logic was, and getting some simple answer, flung myself on the floor and buried myself in it, it has never been in my power to study anything, – mathematics, ethics, metaphysics, gravitation, thermodynamics, optics, chemistry, comparative anatomy, psychology, phonetics, economic, the history of science, whist, men and women, wine, metrology, except as a study of semiotic' (Hardwick 1977: 85–6). We can confidently take 'phonetics' in this catalogue as a *pars pro toto* for what Peirce elsewhere (1:271) certified as 'the vast and splendidly developed science of linguistics.'

Among philosophers, Charles Morris (1946: 220–3, 1964: 60–2) appears to have been the most circumspect about the links between semiotics and linguistics. The suggestion he made in 1946 (Morris 1946: 221), and that I well remember from seminars of his that I had attended six years before that, was that semiotics was to provide 'the metalanguage for linguistics,' and thus that the terminology of linguistics would be defined in semiotic terms. 'The carrying out of this program consistently and in detail would mean the emergence of a semiotically grounded science of linguistics.' Oddly enough, Morris's wish came true, in a way, four years after his death, when Shapiro (1983: ix) made an earnest 'attempt to found a Peircean linguistics ... along lines suggested by Peirce's semeiotic in the context of his entire philosophy.' This shot seems, however, to have misfired, for it was either ignored by workers in the mainstream of linguistics or condemned by other experts on Peirce (Walther 1984: 117). Garver (1986: 74) judged Shapiro's version of semiotics 'unsound, even from a Peircean point of view.' (Actually, Shapiro's approach was anticipated by several other linguists, notably including Uriel Weinreich and Raimo Anttila, but these treatments of linguistic data within a strongly semiotic framework, as Rauch [1987, *passim*] reminds us with characteristic understatement, 'have not provoked a revolution in linguistic method' either.)

Linguistics, Carnap (1942: 13) specified, 'is the descriptive, empirical part of semiotic (of spoken or written languages).' Morris expanded on Carnap's proposition by introducing the very general notion of a *lansign-system*, applicable not only to spoken and written languages but also to mathematics and symbolic logic, 'and perhaps to the arts' (Morris 1964: 60), noting that it is commonly admitted (he mentions, however, only Hjelmslev, Bloomfield, and Greenberg) 'that linguistics is part of semiotic' (1946: 62). His proposal to replace the word 'language' with 'lansign-system' (1946: 36), and associated terminological innovations, proved stillborn; but he was right in observing that most linguists who have given the matter any thought at all did view their discipline as a part of semiotics. Among linguists of this persuasion, Saussure is customarily discussed first.

Saussure, who used the word *semiology* rather than *semiotics* – and sometimes the more apt, yet never espoused, French synonym *signologie* – seems to have devoted very little time in his lectures to thus situating linguistics. A compact, but revered and influential, passage reads as follows:

A language ... is a social institution. But it is in various respects distinct from political, juridical and other institutions. Its special nature emerges when we bring into consideration a different order of facts ... A language is a system of signs expressing ideas [cf. Locke!], and hence comparable to writing, the deaf-and-dumb alphabet, symbolic rites, forms of politeness, military signals, and so on. It is simply the most important of such systems ... It is therefore possible to conceive of a science *which studies the role of signs as part of social life*. It would form part of social psychology, and hence of general psychology. We shall call it *semiology* (from the Greek *semeion*, 'sign'). It would investigate the nature of signs and the laws governing them. Since it does not yet exist, one cannot say for certain that it will exist. But it has the right to exist, a place ready for it in advance. Linguistics is only one branch of this general science. The laws which semiology will discover will be the laws applicable in linguistics, and linguistics will thus be assigned to a clearly defined place in the field of human knowledge. (Saussure 1967: 15–16)

Several essays were subsequently fashioned to carry out the implications of Saussure's program, the first among them being the thoughtful – and too long neglected – attempt of Buyssens (1943: 31), who took it as given that 'seul le point de vue sémiologique permet de déterminer scientifiquement l'objet de la linguistique.' To the principle articulated here, according to which linguistic problems are 'first and foremost semiological,' and the 'need will be felt to consider them as semiological phenomena and to explain them in terms of the laws of semiology' (Saussure 1967: 16–17), another has to be juxtaposed, namely, that linguistics, in Saussure's view, was to serve as the model ('le patron général') for semiology (or semiotics). This formula, by the way, turned out to have been thoroughly mistaken, and fatally misleading for research endeavours, for instance, in such adjacent areas as 'kinesics.'

Sapir (1929: 211) also viewed linguistic facts as 'specialized forms of symbolic behavior,' and he mentioned among 'the primary communicative processes of society ... language; gesture in its widest sense; the imitation of overt behavior; and a large and ill-defined group of implicit processes which grow out of overt behavior and which may be rather vaguely referred to as "social suggestion."' He then added that 'language is the communicative process par excellence in every known society' (Sapir 1931: 78–9). He did not, however, as far as I know, use any term of the 'semiotics' family.

Gardiner (1932: 85) remarks that the 'student of linguistic theory ... treats utterances solely as instruments of communication, as significant signs. His interest is, in fact, what has been variously called semasiology, significs, or semantics. It is a wide field, and when rightly understood, embraces the entire domain of both grammar and lexicography.' Here should be mentioned, as well, Bloomfield's dictum (1939: 255) that 'linguistics is the chief contributor to semiotic'; and Weinreich's (1968: 164), that 'specialized research into natural human [sic] language – the semiotic phenomenon par excellence – constitutes linguistics.' To round out such aphoristic dicta, one might finally cite Greimas and Courtes's (1982: 177) interpretation of what linguistics is: this, they claim, 'may be defined as a scientific study of language as semiotic system' (see further Mounin 1970).

The contributions of two major figures of twentieth-century linguisitics need to be singled out: Hjelmslev's (Trabant 1981) – who was thoroughly influenced by Saussure – and Jakobson's – who was equally permeated by Saussure but far more persuaded by Peirce. Greimas and Courtés (1982: 288), ignoring history altogether, proclaimed that Hjelmslev 'was the first to propose a coherent semiotic theory,' a reckless exaggeration by which they seem to have meant merely that he considered semiotics 'to be a hierarchy ... endowed with a double mode of existence, paradigmatic and syntagmatic ... and provided with at least two articulation planes – expression and content.' Natural semiotic systems then, in Hjelmslev's conception, comprehend natural languages. As Eco (1984: 14) says, Hjelmslev's definition can indeed be taken 'as a more rigorous development of the Saussurean concept,' but it is also the case that his program for semiotics 'so confidently advertised has never been carried out successfully in any domain of science' (Sebeok 1985: 13). Even Trabant (1981: 149) concedes that Hjelmslev's theory has had virtually no impact, even while he tries to show Hjelmslev's originality in the development of modern linguistics in his only partially successful feat of having commingled it with general semiotics.

Jakobson's imput into the doctrine of signs was every bit as pervasive as Hjelmslev's, even though it remains less readily identifiable (it is presented cogently and comprehensively in Eco 1977). Jakobson (1974: 32) concurred with other linguists that 'of these two sciences of man,' to wit, semiotics and linguistics, 'the latter has a narrower scope,' being confined to the communication of verbal messages, 'yet, on the other hand, any human communication of nonverbal messages presupposes a circuit of verbal messages, without a reverse implication.' The point most pertinent to the matter under discussion here is that he unfurled a more all-embracing multi-layered hierarchy of the 'communication disciplines.' (In doing so, he was actually refining a scheme originally put forward by Lévi-Strauss 1958: 95.) According to this wider conception, in any (human) society communication operates on three levels: 'exchange of messages, exchange of utilities (namely goods and services), and exchange of women (or, perhaps, in a more generalizing formulation, exchange of mates). Therefore, linguistics (jointly with the other semiotic disciplines), economics, and finally kinship and marriage studies "approach the same kinds of problems on different strategic levels and really pertain to the same field" ... All these levels of communication assign a fundamental role to language.'

In my view, what vitiates this design is that it is not catholic enough by far; in particular, it fails to take into account the several fundamental divisions of biosemiotics or biocommunication (Tembrock 1971), such as endosemiotics (T. von Uexküll, ed., 1980: 291), zoosemiotics (Sebeok 1963), phytosemiotics (Krampen 1981), and so forth, in none of which does language – an exclusively genus-specific propensity of *Homo* – play any role whatsoever. In short, while elegantly disposing of the chief departments in the 'semiotics of culture,' this scheme fails to account for those of the much broader domains in the 'semiotics of nature' within which all of the foregoing rest embedded. If semiotics is indeed to remain 'the science of communicative sign systems,' semiotics forfeits its immense responsibility for synthesizing linguistics with 'research on animal behavior, particularly signaling systems, and much more' (Lekomcev 1977: 39).

By and large, generative grammarians have paid no heed to semiotics, although Chomsky (1980: 253) himself alludes to a 'science of semiology' in the framework of which, he says, it 'is tempting to draw an analogy ... to rules of grammar, which relate various levels of linguistic representation.' Such a science, he adds, 'may not lie very far beyond the horizons of current inquiry,' noting 'some attempts at a general synthesis.' The compatibility of Chomsky's theory with semiotic views of symbolic function remains to be explored, but will probably find its explanation when both can be integrated into the fabric of a more comprehensive cognitive science.

Verbal and Nonverbal Signing

Jakob von Uexküll's consideration (1982: 4–6) of the relationship between the sign-processes of nature and of language provides a fertile framework for examining verbal and nonverbal signing. The distinction between code and message, or, more narrowly, between *langue* and *parole*, corresponds to von Uexküll's distinction between 'active plan' and 'concrete living existence.' Of the plan, he wrote: 'Our mind possesses an inner plan that reveals itself only in the moment when it starts to be active. Therefore we must observe the mind during the time in which it receives and works out impressions according to its activity.' Also: 'the form is never anything else but the product of a plan imprinted on the indifferent materia that could have taken another form as well.' It should be kept in mind that this great innovator in theoretical biology had never heard of his elder contemporaries, Peirce and Saussure.

A sweeping study of signs and systems of signs, whether verbal or nonverbal, demands both synchronic approaches (structural as well as functional) and an application of diachronic perspectives (developmental or ontogenetic, and evolutionary or phylogenetic (Sebeok 1979: 27–34, 57–60; and 1985: 26–45). As to the ontogeny of semiosis in our species, it is perfectly clear that manifold nonverbal sign systems are 'wired into' the behaviour of every normal neonate; this initial semiosic endowment enables children to survive and to both acquire and compose a working knowledge of their world (*Umwelt*) before they acquire verbal signs (see, for example, Bullowa 1979 and Bruner 1983). The point to keep in mind is that nonverbal sign systems by no means atrophy (though they may, of course, become impaired) in the course of reaching adulthood and old age. In other words, the two repertoires – the chronologically prior and the much, much younger – become and remain profoundly interwoven, to both complement and supplement one another throughout each human individual's life. This reliance on two independent but subtly intertwined semiotic modes – sometimes dubbed zoosemiotic and anthroposemiotic – is

what is distinctively hominid, rather than the mere language propensity characteristic of our species.

When it comes to questions of phylogeny, I have always contended that the emergence of life on earth, some 3.5 billions of
years ago, was tantamount to the advent of semiosis. The life science and the sign science thus mutually imply one another. I have
also argued that the derivation of language out of any animal communication system is an exercise in total futility, because language
did not evolve to subserve humanity's communicative exigencies.
It evolved, as we shall see in the next chapter, as an exceedingly
sophisticated modelling device, in the sense of von Uexküll's
Umweltlehre, as presented, for example, in 1982 (see also Lotman
1977), surely present – that is, language-as-a-modelling-system, not
speech-as-a-communicative-tool – in *Homo habilis*. This ancestral
member of our genus appeared, rather abruptly, only about two
million years ago. Language, which was an evolutionary adaptation
in the genus, became 'exapted' (Gould and Vrba 1982) in the
species *Homo sapiens* a mere three hundred thousand years ago in
the form of speech. It took that long for the encoding abilities of
Homo sapiens to become fine-tuned with our species' corresponding decoding abilities. Note that, as in human ontogeny, verbal
semiosis has by no means replaced the far hoarier diversiform nonverbal manifestations, for reasons that were spelled out and elucidated by Bateson (in Sebeok 1968: 614):

[The] decay of organs and skills under evolutionary replacement is a
necessary and inevitable systemic phenomenon. If, therefore, verbal
language were in any sense an evolutionary replacement of communication by [nonverbal] means ... we would expect the old ... systems to have
undergone conspicuous decay. Clearly they have not. Rather, the [non-
verbal sign uses] of men have become richer and more complex, and
[nonverbal communication] has blossomed side by side with the
evolution of verbal language.

In sum, a preponderance of expert opinion persuades that linguistics is a structurally rather than functionally autonomous
branch of semiotics, the rest of which encompasses a wide variety

of nonverbal systems of signification and communication which, in humans, flourish side by side with the former, related in reciprocity. In the longitudinal time section, whether in the life of organisms or the lives of men and women, nonverbal semiosis has substantial primacy. Studies of precisely how verbal and nonverbal signs intermingle with and modify each other in our multiform speech communities must be further considered conjointly by linguists and other semioticians.

All living beings interact by means of nonverbal message exchanges. Normal adult human beings interact by *both* nonverbal *and* verbal message exchanges. Although the latter, namely, language, is a semi-autonomous structure, it does lie embedded in a labyrinthine matrix of other varieties of semiotic patterns used among us and variously inherited from our animal ancestry. 'Since,' as Jakobson (1974: 39) emphasized, 'verbal messages analyzed by linguists are linked with communication of non-verbal messages,' and since, as Benveniste (1971: 14) insisted, 'language is also human; it is the point of interaction between the mental and cultural life in man,' efficacious language teaching should be regarded as an endeavour in what Morris (1946: 353–4) has called 'applied semiotic [which] utilizes knowledge about signs for the accomplishment of various purposes.' The question that I would like to repeat here (raised in Sebeok 1985: 179) is this: 'if, as is the case, we lavish incalculable amounts of energy, time, and money to instil in children and adults a range of foreign language competencies, why are the indissolubly parallel foreign gesticulatory skills all but universally neglected, especially considering that even linguists are fully aware that what has been called the total communication package, "best likened to a coaxial cable carrying many messages at the same time," is hardly an exaggerated simile?'

When I first asked this question, actually in 1975, very sparse materials existed for training in foreign gesticulatory skills; those that did were restricted to French and Spanish (Iberian, Columbian). Today, the situation has ameliorated, but not by much. The impact of nonverbal behaviour on foreign-language teaching was reviewed by Ward and von Raffler-Engel (1980: 287–304), but their essay described the results of a very modest experiment. Beginning in the late 1970s, the Research Center for Language and Semiotic Studies at Indiana University began to give this manifest lack of material some preliminary attention (the project was described in Johnson 1979 and in Wintsch 1979). Johnson also completed a handbook on nonverbal communication for teachers of Japanese, which was accompanied by a widely used half-hour film, in which native Japanese perform specific gestures as well as situational interactions (see also Tsuda 1984). Johnson likewise prepared a corresponding handbook for teachers of Gulf Arabic. Harrison (1983) published a parallel handbook comparing Brazilian and North American social behaviour, while Rector and Trinta (1985) produced an illustrated manual on nonverbal communication, that is, gesturing, also in Brazil. All this, however, can only be deemed a mere beginning in what needs to be accomplished worldwide, and especially in the production of indispensable visual aids.

9

Language as a Primary Modelling System?

The expression 'primary modelling system' – coupled, as a rule, with the contrasting concept 'secondary modelling system,' which emphasizes its derivational character in relation to natural language – has been central to Russian semiotics of the Moscow-Tartu school since 1962, when it was proposed by Zaliznyak, Ivanov, and Toporov (see Lucid 1977: 47–58 and Rudy 1986). In 1974 I interpreted the inferred concept – having checked my provisional understanding, when I gave a lecture at the University of Tartu in August 1970 with Professor Ivanov – as follows: 'The notion of a secondary modeling system, in the broad sense, refers to an ideological model of the world where the environment stands in reciprocal relationship with some other system, such as an individual organism, a collectivity, a computer, or the like, and where its reflection functions as a control of this system's total mode of communication. A model of the world thus constitutes a program for the behavior of the individual, the collectivity, the machine, etc., since it defines its choice of operations, as well as the rules and motivations underlying them. A model of the world can be actualized in the various forms of human behavior and its products, including linguistic texts – hence the emphasis on the verbal arts – social institutions, movements of civilization, and so forth' (Sebeok 1985: 23). Although Ivanov graciously acquiesced at the time to my ad hoc formulation, this, in retrospect, seems to me to require further elucidation. Accordingly, the purpose of this final chapter is to zero in on the human modelling system *par excellence* – verbal language.

Modelling System

The canonical definition of a modelling system was framed by Lotman in 1967 (Lucid 1977: 7) as 'a structure of elements and of rules for combining them that is in a state of fixed analogy to the entire sphere of an object of knowledge, insight or regulation. Therefore a modeling system can be regarded as a language. Systems that have a natural language as their basis and that acquire supplementary superstructures, thus creating languages of a second level, can appropriately be called secondary modeling systems.' Natural language, in brief, is thus posited as the primary, or basic, infrastructure for all other human sign systems; and the latter – such as myth or religion – are held to be resultant superstructures constructed upon the former. In 1971 Lotman and Uspenski (in English 1978) elaborated their view of the semiotic study of culture, noting that, in their scheme, language is viewed as carrying out a specific communicative function by providing the collective with a presumption of communicability.

An underlying question concerns, more generally, the concept of 'model' – which is essentially a reductive analogy, and therefore ultimately a kind of icon – and its applications, if any, as a technical term in semiotics of the nonverbal and the verbal in particular. Certainly, it is a fashionable appellation in the literature and philosophy of science, where it has acquired, however, many different connotations. Some of the more important of these – notably in logic, mathematics, and physics – are provocatively discussed by Hesse (1967).

The only recorded discussion of linguistic models that I am aware of took place at the 1960 International Congress for Logic, Methodology and Philosophy of Science, with the participation (among others) of Bar-Hillel and Chomsky. The proceedings include a highly useful, although neglected, paper by Yuen Ren Chao, which correctly notes that, while 'the term "model" is relatively new in linguistics ... the use of what may reasonably be regarded as models is as old as the study of language' (Chao 1962: 558; for later references, see Welte 1974: 1:386–7, Stewart 1976, Koch 1986). Chao claims that the earliest mention of models in linguistics was in 1944 by Z.S. Harris. The term was thereafter used with increasing frequency, yet in a bewildering variety of senses:

Chao lists no less than thirty synonyms or more or less equivalent phrases of 'model' for the fourteen years he surveyed. But none of these seems to conform to, or possess the scope of, the uses of 'model' in the Russian tradition.

Some twentieth-century pre-Chao and post-Chao models of semiosis are illustrated by the following graphic displays, a modest sample chosen almost at random out of a far larger number (Fiske 1982). It should also be noted that these models are all, more of less, linked intertextually among one another; namely, their framers were aware of earlier models and their interpretations of these models were repositioned in the light of each later model.

This 'convenient diagram of Symbol, Reference and Referent' was created in the 1920s by Ogden and Richards (1923: 11):

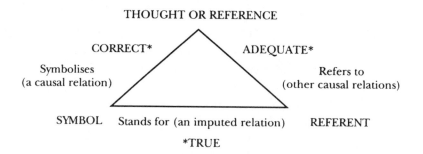

In Europe, the following 'organon model' of language by Bühler (1934: 28) became widely influential after the mid-1930s:

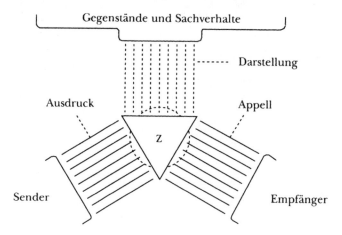

Shannon and Weaver's (1949: 5) schematic flow chart, representing a general communication system, has become a classic that keeps getting copied with all sorts of variations, for it is heuristically valuable and suggests ways of explaining the theory embedded in it:

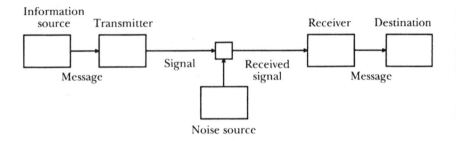

In the early 1960s, I (1972a: 14) tried to depict by way of a Morley Triangle the relationships between Bühler's model and Jakobson's (1960: 253, 257) more comprehensive information-theoretical schema of six constitutive factors, each of which is posited to determine a different function of language; this was, in turn, actuated by the Shannon and Weaver model:

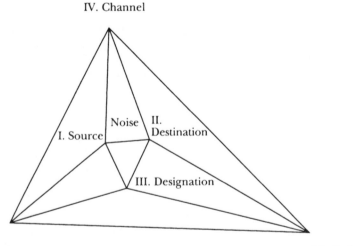

Chao does not press his own views, but it is clear that, had he developed them, they would have mirrored common semiotic principles by changing their parity. What he does say is that, in his model of models, 'there are things and models of things, the latter being also things but used in a special way' (1962: 564). One would nowadays rather say that there are objects and signs of objects, the former also being signs but used in a special way.

Chao then gives this example: 'If we take any two things, say cabbages and kings, and make, say, a cabbage the model of a king, there is not likely to be much that is true of one that is also true of the other, though usually not zero, e.g. both are living things or can be, etc., but the modelity of cabbages with respect to kings is fairly low.'

This can be rephrased in standard semiotic idiom in this way: a cabbage (*aliquid*) stands for (*stat pro*) a king (*aliquo*). If it is likely that much of what is true of one (i.e., of the sign 'cabbage') is also true of the other (i.e., of the object 'king'), then perhaps one might amplify, with Peirce (2:257), that the cabbage tends to be a Dicent Sinsign, involving both 'an iconic Sinsign to embody the information and a Rhematic Indexical Sinsign to indicate the Object to which the information refers.' However, if very little is true of one that is also true of the other (even though it is not zero), one might say, again with Peirce (2:261) that the cabbage tends to be a Rhematic Symbol or a Symbolic Rheme, such as a common noun. In Jakobson's (1980: 11, 22) much simplified version of semiosis, a model м, a cabbage, could be said to function as a *renvoi* of the thing т, a king, and this referral could, by virtue of an effective similarity, be iconic – after all, as Morris (1971: 273) taught us, iconicity is 'a matter of degree.' Or, by virtue of an imputed, conventional, habitual contiguity, the referral could be symbolic, much as, for the experimental dog in the Pavlovian paradigm, the sound of a metronome became an arbitrarily paired symbol (i.e., a conditioned reflex) for dry food.

Uexküll's Model Revisited

Russian conceptions of models and modelling systems clearly owe much to Jakob von Uexküll's theory of meaning (Gipper 1963,

Sebeok 1979) developed in Hamburg during the first four decades of this century, by this great biologist, in a series of sagacious if quirky contributions to semiotics. Stepanov (1971: 27–32), for instance, singles him out for extended mention in the course of his sketch of (then) current trends in modern (bio)semiotics.

Uexküll's highly original *Umwelt-Forschung* – which its creator viewed as a scientific theory anchored in Kant's a priori intuitions – is truly a fundamental theory as much of sign-processes (or semiosis) as of vital functions. Moreover, his conception at once *utilizes* a pivotal model – the famous 'function cycle.' This simple, albeit not linear, diagram, by which, as Lorenz (1971: 274) noted, 'a vast programme of research is implied,' in itself *constitutes* a cybernetic theory of modelling so fundamental that the evolution of language cannot be grasped without it. His functional cycle looks like this:

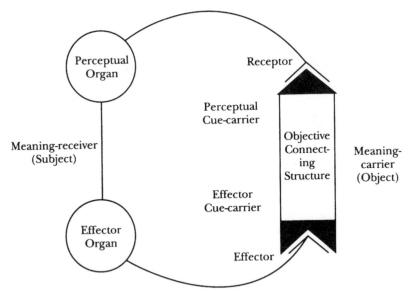

The term.*Umwelt* has proved notoriously recalcitrant to translation, although 'subjective universe,' 'phenomenal world,' and 'self-world' variously approximate the author's intent. However, 'model' renders it more incisively, especially in view of his credo that 'every subject is the constructor of its Umwelt' (Uexküll 1982: 87).

As Jacob (1982: 55) has explained with utmost clarity, 'every organism is so equipped as to obtain a certain perception of the outer world. Each species thus lives in its own unique sensory world, to which other species may be partially or totally blind ... What an organism detects in its environment is always but a part of what is around. And this part differs according to the organism.' The world-as-perceived depends crucially on each organism's total sensorium and on the way its brain integrates sensory with motor events. But the inclusive behavioural resources of any organism must be reasonably aligned with its model of 'reality' (*Natur*), that is, the system of signs its nervous system is capable of assembling – or it will surely be doomed, by natural selection, to extinction.

Schneirla's (1965) biphasic approach/withdrawal theory furnishes a *minimal model* which must have been crucial for the survival of all animal types, from protozoans to primates (including humans). Such a miniature model – or 'modelita,' in Chao's (1962: 565) sobriquet – evidently requires much the same organs, but is played out in two functionally opposed systems, one for the reaching of food and mates, the other for the evasion of noxious situations. A key postulate of this holistic oppositive A/W theory, allowing, as it does, for plasticity through experience, is that it cyclically relates every organism's *Innenwelt*, 'comprising,' as Lorenz (1971: 275) explains, 'the whole bodily structures and/or functions, to its characteristic habitat, *Umgebung*, or observer's *Umwelt*' (after Uexküll 1909).

The *Innenwelt* of every animal comprises a model – whether of a minimal A/W type or of a more elaborate kind – that is made up of an elementary array of several types of nonverbal signs (variously elaborated by Uexküll [1982: 10–11] under which such labels as *Ordnungszeichen, Inhaltszeichen, Lokalzeichen, Richtungszeichen, Wirkzeichen*, and the like). Solely in the genus Homo have verbal signs emerged. To put it another way, only hominids possess two mutually sustaining repertoires of signs, the zoosemiotic nonverbal, plus, superimposed, the anthroposemiotic verbal. The latter is the modelling system which the Russian scholars call primary, but which, in truth, is phylogenetically as well as ontogenetically secondary to the nonverbal; and, therefore, what they call 'secondary' is actually a further, tertiary augmentation of the former. The congruity of this expanded paradigm with Popper's (see Eccles 1979) famous Worlds 1–2–3 model is unmistakable: his World 3 is the world of culture; his World 2, 'the other uniquely human world' (Eccles 1979: 115–16), explicitly encompassing language and developing together with the former 'in some kind of symbiotic interaction'; and his World 1 is the whole material world of the cosmos, both inorganic and organic, including machines and all of biology.

Language as a Modelling System

The earliest known species in the genus *Homo* is the form Louis Leakey named *habilis*, first described in 1964, and now usually regarded as a short-lived transitional African form, of some two million years ago, ancestral to all the later hominid species. With a brain capacity of 600–800 cc, this ancestral creature must have had a mute verbal modelling device lodged in its brain, but it could not encode it in articulate, linear speech. Language is, in fact, among its quintessential taxonomic markers (in conjunction with chipped pebbles and clusters of animal bone that evince deliberate cutting and breaking).

The evolutionary success of *habilis* is corroborated by the very swift appearance, a mere half a million years later, of the succeeding species, *H. erectus*, with a brain volume of 800–1,200 cc; this speedy attainment is undoubtedly due to the species' linguistic competence, also indirectly manifested by its possession of tool kits exhibiting standardized design, the use of fire, and its rapid global dispersion.

Starting around three hundred thousand years ago, an archaic form of *H. sapiens* evolved out of the erectus species, with a growth of skull capacity up to 1,400 cc, and many concurrent novelties. It is reasonable to conclude that this pre-modern human already had the capacity to encode language into speech and the concomitant ability to decode it at the other end of the communication loop. *H. sapiens* appeared a mere forty thousand years ago, with brains averaging 1,500 cc.

The cardinal points of this brief scenario are twofold: *language evolved as an adaptation; whereas speech developed out of language as a derivative 'exaptation'* over a succeeding period of approximately two million years. These twin propositions need to be made plain with reference to a suggestion by Gould and Vrba (1982). These authors emphasize the distinction between historical genesis and current utility, suggesting that characteristics which evolved for other uses (or none) may later come to be co-opted for their current role. The former operation is customarily called *adaptation*; for the latter, they propose a new designation, *exaptation*.

Accordingly, languages – consisting of a set of features that promotes fitness – can best be thought of as having been built by selection for the cognitive function of modelling, and, as the philosopher Popper and the linguist Chomsky have likewise insisted, not at all for the message-swapping function of communication. The latter was routinely carried on by nonverbal means, as in all animals, as it continues to be in the context of most human interactions today.

Several million years later, however, language came to be 'exapted' for communication, first in the form of speech (and later of script, and so forth). This relatively brief elapsed time was required for a plausible mutual adjustment of the encoding with the decoding capacity, but, since absolute mutual comprehension remains a distant goal, the system continues to be fine-tuned and tinkered with. Gould and Vrba (1982: 13) give many interesting examples of comparable biological processes, stressing that current utility carries no automatic implication about historical origin, and concluding with the empirical observation that 'most of what the brain does now to enhance our survival lies in the domain of exaptation.' The common flaw in much evolutionary reasoning – the inference of historical genesis from current utility – egregiously contaminated virtually all research in the nineteenth century and even quite recently has confounded the problem of the origin of language, which has therefore proved intractable to most probes based on unbiological principles.

It is interesting that in the other universal domain of human modelling where nonverbal – or, as Bullowa (1979: 9–10) terms it, 'extra-verbal' – communication clearly has exclusive primacy over language, to wit, in ontogenesis, the identical marring feature – namely, 'our habit of thinking of communication consisting mainly of language' – 'has delayed the study of the earliest human communication.'

Concluding Remarks

As Peirce (1:538) taught us, 'Every thought is a sign,' but as he also wrote, 'Not only is thought in the organic world, but it develops there' (5:551). Every mental model is, of course, also a sign; and not only is modelling an indispensable characteristic of the human world, but it also permeates the entire organic world, where, indeed, it developed. The animals' *milieu extérieur* and *milieu intérieur,* as well as the feedback links between them, are created and sustained by such models. A model in this general sense is a semiotic production with carefully stated assumptions and rules for biological and logical operations.

This is as true of bees (Peirce 5:551) as it is, on a far vaster scale, of Isaac Newton's and Albert Einstein's grand models of the universe. Einstein constructed his model out of nonverbal signs, 'of visual and some of muscular type,' and laboured long and hard 'only in a secondary stage' to transmute this creation into 'conventional words and other signs,' so that he could communicate it to others. 'The words or the language, as they are written or spoken,' Einstein wrote in a letter to Hadamard (1945: 142–3), 'do not seem to play any role in my mechanism of thought. The physical entities which seem to serve as elements in thought are certain signs and more or less clear images which can be "voluntarily" reproduced and combined.'

As we have seen throughout this book, the relatively simple, nonverbal models that animals live by and that normal human infants likewise employ are more or less pliable representations which, as we saw, must fit 'reality' sufficiently to tend to secure their survival in their ecological niche (an ethological expression which, in semiotic parlance, refers to the *Umwelt* as viewed by an observer of the subject under scrutiny). Such 'top-down' modelling (to use a current jargon borrowed from the cognitive sciences) can persist and become very sophisticated indeed in the adult life of exceptionally gifted individuals, as borne out by Einstein's testimonial or by what we know about Mozart's or Picasso's abilities to model intricate auditory or visual compositions in their heads in anticipation of transcribing them onto paper or canvas. This kind of nonverbal modelling is indeed primary, in both a phylogenetic and an onto-genetic sense.

Language itself is, properly speaking, a secondary modelling system, by virtue of the all-but-singular fact that it incorporates a syntactic component (for there is, as far as we know, no other such component in zoosemiotic systems, although this feature does abound in endosemiotic systems, such as the genetic code, the immune code, the metabolic code, and the neural code). Syntax makes it possible for hominids not only to represent immediate 'reality' (in the sense discussed above), but also, uniquely among animals, to frame an indefinite number of possible worlds.

Hence humanity is able to fabricate tertiary modelling systems of the sort Bonner (1980: 186), for instance, calls 'true culture,' requiring 'a system of representing all the subtleties of language,' in contrast to 'nonhuman culture,' and thereby produce what the Moscow-Tartu group has traditionally been calling a 'secondary modelling system.' It is on this level, redefined now as tertiary, that nonverbal and verbal sign assemblages blend together in the most creative modelling that nature has thus far evolved.

Glossary

The following glossary contains the main technical terms used in this book.

Abduction process by which a new concept is formed on the basis of an existing concept which is perceived as having something in common with it

Abstract concept a mental form whose external referent cannot be demonstrated or observed directly

Adaptor bodily movement indicating or satisfying some emotional state or need: e.g., scratching one's head when puzzled, rubbing one's forehead when worried

Affect displays hand movements and facial expressions communicating emotional meaning

Alliteration the repetition of the initial consonant sounds or features of words

Anthroposemiosis semiosis in humans

Anthroposemiotics the study of semiosis, modelling, and representation in humans

Artefact an object produced or shaped by human craft, especially a tool, a weapon, or an ornament of archaeological or historical interest

Artefactual media media such as books, paintings, sculptures, letters, etc. made by human beings in order to transmit messages

Artificial model a model produced artificially, i.e., intentionally, by a human being

Binary opposition	minimal difference between two forms
Biosemiotics	branch of semiotics which aims to study semiosis, modelling, and representation in all life forms
Bipedalism	walking upright on two feet
Channel	the physical means by which a signal or message is transmitted
Code	system of signifying elements which can be deployed to represent types of phenomena in specific ways
Coevolution	the sociobiological theory that genes and culture are evolving in tandem
Cognitive style	the particular way in which information and knowledge are processed
Communication	capacity to participate with other organisms in the reception and processing of specific kinds of signals
Concept	mental form
Concrete concept	mental form whose external referent is demonstrable and observable in a direct way
Connotation	extension of a form over a new meaning domain that is recognized as entailing the features of the form by implication
Connotative extensional modelling	the process of extending the meanings of primary forms to encompass connotative meanings
Connotatum	extended meaning of a form
Context	situation – physical, psychological, and social – in which a form is used or occurs, or to which it refers
Conventional sign	sign that has no apparent connection to any perceivable feature of its referent
Culture	the system of daily living that is held together by a signifying order (signs, codes, texts, connective forms)
Decoding	use of a code to decipher forms
Deixis	process of referring to something by pointing it out or specifying it in some way
Denotation	initial, or intensional, meaning captured by a form
Denotatum	the initial signified of a sign

Diachronicity	change in a form over time
Distinctive feature	minimal element that makes up a form and which singularly or in combination with other distinctive features serves to differentiate its meaning from that of other forms
Drive	the innate impulse informing animals when to migrate, when (and how) to court one another, when to feed their young, and so on
Emblems	gestures that directly translate words or phrases: e.g., the *Okay* sign, the *Come here* sign
Encoding	use of a code to make forms
Ethology	the study of animals in their natural habitats
Extensionality	process of extending the physical constitution or meaning of forms
Extensional modelling	the extension of primary models both morphologically and connotatively for further representational uses
Externalized form	form made to stand for something
Fetish	an object that is believed to have magical or spiritual, powers, or which can cause sexual arousal
Firstness	earliest strategy for knowing an object with the senses
Form	a mental image, or an external representation of something
Gesture	use of the hands, the arms, and, to a lesser extent, the head to make bodily forms of all kinds
Icon	sign form which simulates its referent in some way
Iconicity	the process of representing referents with iconic forms
Index	sign form which establishes a contiguity with its referent (pointing it out, showing its relation to other things, etc.)
Indexicality	process of representing referents with indexical signs
Induction	process of deriving a concept from particular facts or instances

Inflection	variations or changes that words undergo to indicate their relations with other words
Innenwelt	the world of internal experiences of a species
Internal model	mental form, mental image
Intertextuality	referents present in one text which allude to referents in other texts
Language	verbal semiosis and representation
Map	a representation, usually on a plane surface, of a region of the earth
Meaning	particular concept elicited by a specific representational form
Medium	technical or physical means by which a message is transmitted
Mental image	mental outline of something (a shape, a sound, etc.)
Metonymy	use of an entity to refer to another that is related to it
Mimesis	intentional making of forms in a simulative manner; in a phrase, intentional (witting) simulation
Mode	manner in which a form is encoded (visual, auditory, etc.)
Model	form that has been imagined or made externally (through some physical medium) to stand for an object, event, feeling, etc.
Modelling	the innate ability to produce forms to represent objects, events, feelings, actions, situations, and ideas perceived to have some meaning, purpose, or useful function
Modelling principle	principle claiming that representation is a de facto modelling process
Modelling systems theory	theory which posits the presence of species-specific modelling systems that allow a species to produce the forms it needs for understanding the world in its own way
Motor program	self-contained circuit able to direct the coordinated movements of many different muscles to accomplish a task

Myth	any story or narrative that aims to explain the origin of something
Mythology	the study of myths
Name	form that identifies a human being or, by connotative extension, an animal, an object (such as a commercial product), or event (such as a hurricane)
Narrative	something told or written, such as an account, story, tale, etc.
Narrator	the teller of the narrative
Natural form	form produced by nature
Natural media	natural media of communication such as the voice (speech), the face (expressions), and the body (gesture, posture, etc.)
Novel	a fictional prose narrative of considerable length, typically having a plot that is unfolded by the actions, speech, and thoughts of the characters
Onomastics	the study of names
Onomatopoeia	vocal iconicity (*drip, boom,* etc.)
Opposition	process by which forms are differentiated through a minimal change in their signifiers
Osmosis	the spontaneous production of a simulative form in response to some stimulus or need
Paradigmaticity	a differentiation property of forms
Personal deixis	process of referring to the relations that exist among participants taking part in a situation
Phoneme	minimal unit of sound in a language that allows its users to differentiate word meanings
Phylogenesis	the development of all semiosic abilities (iconicity, symbolism, language, etc.) in the human species
Phytosemiosis	semiosis in plants
Phytosemiotics	the study of semiosis in plants
Primary model	simulative form (icon)
Primary model-ling system	instinctive ability to model the *sensible* properties of things (i.e. properties that can be *sensed*)

Programmed learning	the ability of a species to learn only those things that are relevant to its life needs
Referent	an object, event, feeling, idea, etc. that is represented by a form
Referential domain	a class of objects, events, feelings, ideas, etc. represented by a form
Regulator	gesticulant regulating the speech of an interlocutor: e.g., hand movements indicating *Keep going, Slow down,* etc.
Representation	process of ascribing a form to some referent
Secondary model	either an extension of the physical form or meaning of a simulacrum or an indexical form
Secondary modelling system	system that allows for indication or the extension of forms
Secondness	ability to refer to objects through indication or verbal reference
Semiosis	capacity of a species to produce and comprehend the specific types of models it requires for processing and codifying perceptual input in its own way
Semiotics	the doctrine of signs
Sign	something that stands for something else
Signal	sign that naturally or conventionally (artificially) triggers some reaction on the part of a receiver
Signification	relation that holds between a form and its referent
Signified	part of a sign that is referred to (the referent)
Signifier	part of a sign that does the referring (the form)
Sign stimulus (releaser)	cue that enables animals to recognize a critical referent when they encounter it for the first time
Simulacrum	simulated form
Spatial deixis	process of referring to the spatial locations of referents
Speech	expressed language
Structuralism	the approach in semiotics that views signs as reflexes of intellectual and emotional structures in the human psyche
Structure	any repeatable or predictable aspect of models
Subordinate concept	concept needed for specialized purposes

Superordinate concept	concept with a highly general referential function
Symbol	sign form that stands arbitrarily or conventionally for its referent
Symbolicity	the process of representing referents with symbolic forms
Symbolism	symbolic meaning in general
Symptom	natural sign which alerts an organism to the presence of altered states in its body
Synchronicity	refers to the fact that forms are constructed at a given point in time for some particular purpose or function
Syndrome	configuration of symptoms with a fixed denotatum
Syntagmaticity	combinatory property of forms
Syntax	syntagmatic structure in language
Temporal deixis	process of referring to the temporal relations that exist among things and events
Tertiary model	a symbolically devised form
Tertiary modelling system	modelling system that undergirds highly abstract, symbol-based modelling
Text	something put together to represent complex (non-unitary) referents
Thirdness	abstract form of knowing
Transmission	the sending and reception of messages
Umwelt	domain that a species is capable of modelling (the external world of experience to which a species has access)
Zoosemiosis	semiosis in animals
Zoosemiotics	the study of semiosis in animals

Bibliography

The following list includes both the works cited in this book and, more generally, some works that have constituted the reference backbone to the various topics treated. It can thus be consulted as a general reading list.

Alston, W.P. (1967a). Religion. *The Encyclopedia of Philosophy* 7: 140–145.
– (1967b). Language. *The Encyclopedia of Philosophy* 4: 384–386.
– (1967c). Sign and Symbol. *The Encyclopedia of Philosophy* 7: 437–441.
Anderson, M., and Merrell, F. (1991). *On Semiotic Modeling.* Berlin: Mouton de Gruyter.
Appelbaum, D. (1990). *Voice.* Albany: State University of New York Press.
Ardrey, R. (1966). *The Territorial Imperative.* New York: Atheneum.
Argyle, M. (1988). *Bodily Communication.* New York: Methuen.
Argyle, M., and Cook, M. (1976). *Gaze and Mutual Gaze.* Cambridge: Cambridge University Press.
Aristotle. (1952). *Poetics.* In *The Works of Aristotle,* vol. 11, ed. W.D. Ross. Oxford: Clarendon Press.
Armstrong, E.A. (1965). *Bird Display and Behaviour.* New York: Dover.
Armstrong, R.L. (1965). John Locke's 'Doctrine of Signs': A New Metaphysics. *Journal of the History of Ideas* 26: 369–382.
Arnheim, R. (1969). *Visual Thinking.* Berkeley: University of California Press.
Ayer, A.J. (1968). *The Origins of Pragmatism: Studies in the Philosophy of Charles Sanders Peirce and William James.* London: Macmillan.

Baer, E. (1982). The Medical Symptom: Phylogeny and Ontogeny. *American Journal of Semiotics* 1: 17–34.

Baigrie, B.S., ed. (1996). *Picturing Knowledge: Historical and Philosophical Problems Concerning the Use of Art in Science*. Toronto: University of Toronto Press.

Bal, M. (1985). *Narratology: Introduction to the Theory of the Narrative*. Toronto: University of Toronto Press.

Bally, C. (1939). Qu'est-ce qu'un signe? *Journal de Psychologie Normale et Pathologique* 112: 161–174.

Bar-Hillel, Y. (1954). Indexical Expressions. *Mind* 63: 359–379.

– (1970). *Aspects of Language*. Jerusalem: The Magnes Press.

Barthes, R. (1957). *Mythologies*. Paris: Seuil.

– (1964). *Éléments de sémiologie*. Paris: Seuil.

– (1967). *Elements of Semiology*. New York: Hill and Wang.

– (1972). Sémiologie et médicine. In *Les sciences de folie*, ed. R. Bastide, 37–46. Paris: Mouton.

Barwise, J., and Perry, J. (1983). *Situations and Attitudes*. Cambridge, Mass.: MIT Press.

Bateson, G. (1968). *Animal Communication: Techniques of Study and Results of Research*. Bloomington: Indiana University Press.

Baudrillard, J. (1981). *For a Critique of the Political Economy of the Sign*. St Louis: Telos Press.

Becker, N., and Schorsch, E. (1975). Geldfetischismus. In *Ergebnisse zur Sexualforschung*, ed. E. Schorsch and G. Schmidt, 238–256. Cologne: Wissenschafts-Verlag.

Behan, R.J. (1926). *Pain: Its Origin, Conduction, Perception, and Diagnostic Significance*. New York: Appleton.

Bemporad, J., Dunton, D., and Spady, F.H. (1976). Treatment of a Child Foot Fetishist. *American Journal of Psychotherapy* 30: 303–316.

Benveniste, E. (1971). *Problems in General Linguistics*. Coral Gables: University of Miami Press.

Berg, H.C. (1976). Does the Flagellar Rotary Motor Step? *Cell Motility* 3: 47–56.

Berger, J. (1972). *Ways of Seeing*. Harmondsworth: Penguin.

Berlin, B., and Kay, P. (1969). *Basic Color Terms*. Berkeley: University of California Press.

Bernardelli, A., ed. (1997). *The Concept of Intertextuality Thirty Years On: 1967–1997*. Special Issue of *Versus* 77/78. Milan: Bompiani.

Bickerton, D. (1981). *The Roots of Language*. Ann Arbor: Karoma Publishers.

– (1990). *Language and Species*. Chicago: University of Chicago Press.

Bilz, R. (1940). *Pars pro toto*. Leipzig: Georg Thieme.

Birdwhistell, R. (1970). *Kinesics and Context: Essays on Body Motion Communication*. Harmondsworth: Penguin.

Black, M. (1962). *Models and Metaphors*. Ithaca: Cornell University Press.

Bloomfield, L. (1933). *Language*. New York: Holt.

– (1939). Linguistic Aspects of Science. *International Encyclopedia of Unified Science* 1: 215–278.

Bonner, J.T. (1980). *The Evolution of Culture in Animals*. Princeton: Princeton University Press.

Bornet, J. (1892). *Early Greek Philosophy*. London: Macmillan.

Bouissac, P. (1985). *Circus and Culture: A Semiotic Approach*. London: University Press of America

Bouissac, P., et al., eds. (1986). *Iconicity: Essays on the Nature of Culture*. Tübingen: Stauffenberg.

Boysson-Bardies, B. de, and Vihman, M.M. (1991). Adaptation to Language: Evidence from Babbling and First Words in Four Languages. *Language* 67: 297–319.

Braten, S. (1988). Dialogic Mind: The Infant and the Adult in Protoconversation. In *Nature, Cognition, and System I*, ed. E. Carvallo, 187–205. Dordrecht: Kluwer.

Bremer, J., and Roodenburg, H., ed. (1991). *A Cultural History of Gesture*. Ithaca: Cornell University Press.

Brodsky, J. (1989). Isaiah Berlin at Eighty. *New York Review of Books* 36: 44–45.

Bronowski, J. (1967). Human and Animal Language. In *To Honor Roman Jakobson*, 374–394. The Hague: Mouton.

Brosses, C. de. (1760). *La culte des dieux fétiches*. Paris.

Brown, R. (1958). *Words and Things*. Glencoe, Ill.: Free Press.

Brown, R.W. (1970). *Psycholinguistics*. New York: Free Press.

Bühler, K. (1908 [1951]). On Thought Connection. In *Organization and Pathology of Thought*, ed. D. Rapaport, 81–92. New York: Columbia University Press.

– (1934). *Sprachtheorie: Die Darstellungsfunktion der Sprache.* Jena: Fischer.

Bullowa, M., ed. (1979). *Before Speech: The Beginning of Interpersonal Communication.* Cambridge: Cambridge University Press.

Burkhardt, D., et al. (1967). *Signals in the Animal World.* New York: McGraw-Hill.

Bursill-Hall, G.L. (1963). Some Remarks on Deixis. *Canadian Journal of Linguistics* 8: 82–96.

Butler, C. (1970). Chemical Communication in Insects: Behavioral and Ecological Aspects. *Communication by Chemical Signals* 1: 35–78.

Buyssens, E. (1943). *Les langages et le discours.* Brussels: Office de Publicité.

Carnap, R. (1942). *Introduction to Semantics.* Cambridge, Mass.: Harvard University Press.

– (1956 [1947]). *Meaning and Necessity: A Study in Semantics and Modal Logic.* Chicago: University of Chicago Press.

Carpenter, C.R. (1969). Approaches to Studies of the Naturalistic Communicative Behavior in Nonhuman Primates. In *Approaches to Animal Communication*, ed. T.A. Sebeok et al., 40–70. The Hague: Mouton.

Cassirer, E.A. (1944). *An Essay on Man: An Introduction to a Philosophy of Human Culture.* New Haven: Yale University Press.

– (1946). *Language and Myth.* New York: Dover.

– (1957). *The Philosophy of Symbolic Forms.* New Haven: Yale University Press.

Celon, E., and Marcus, S. (1973). Le diagnostic comme langage (I). *Cahiers de Linguistique* 10: 163–173.

Chadwick, J., and Mann, W.N. (1950). *The Medical Works of Hippocrates.* Oxford: Blackwell.

Chamberlain, E.N., and Ogilvie, C. (1974). *Symptoms and Signs in Clinical Medicine.* Bristol: Wright.

Chao, Y.R. (1962). Models in Linguistics and Models in General. In *Logic, Methodology, and the Philosophy of Science*, ed. E. Nagel, P. Suppes, and A. Tarski, 558–566. Stanford: Stanford University Press.

– (1968). *Language and Symbolic Systems.* Cambridge: Cambridge University Press.

Cheraskin, E., and Rinsdorf, W. (1973). *Predictive Medicine: A Study in Strategy.* Mountainview, Calif.: Pacific Press.

Cherry, C. (1966). *On Human Communication.* Cambridge, Mass.: MIT Press.

Cherwitz, R., and Hikins, J. (1986). *Communication and Knowledge: An Investigation in Rhetorical Epistemology.* Columbia, SC: University of South Carolina Press.

Chomsky, N. (1957). *Syntactic Structures.* The Hague: Mouton.

– (1976). On the Nature of Language. In *Origins and Evolution of Language and Speech,* ed. H.B. Steklis, S.R. Harnad, and J. Lancaster, 46–57. New York: New York Academy of Sciences.

– (1980). *Rules and Representations.* New York: Columbia University Press.

– (1986). *Knowledge of Language: Its Nature, Origin, and Use.* New York: Praeger.

Clarke, D.S. (1987). *Principles of Semiotic.* London: Routledge and Kegan.

Colby, K.M., and McGuire, M.T. (1981). Signs and Symptoms. *The Sciences* 21: 21–23.

Colton, H. (1983). *The Gift of Touch.* New York: Putnam.

Copeland, J.E., ed. (1984). *New Directions in Linguistics and Semiotics.* Houston: Rice University Studies.

Coseriu, E. (1967). L'arbitraire du signe: Zur Spätgeschichte eines aristotelischen Begriffes. *Archiv für das Studium der Neueren Sprachen und Literaturen* 204: 81–112.

Count, E.W. (1969). Animal Communication in Man-Science. In *Approaches to Animal Communication,* ed. T.A. Sebeok et al., 71–130. The Hague: Mouton.

Crookshank, F.G. (1925). The Importance of a Theory of Signs and a Critique of Language in the Study of Medecine. In *The Meaning of Meaning,* ed. C.K. Ogden and I.A. Richards, Supplement II. London: Kegan Paul.

Crystal, D. (1987). *The Cambridge Encyclopedia of Language.* Cambridge: Cambridge University Press.

Culler, J. (1983). *Roland Barthes.* New York: Oxford University Press.

Danesi, M. (2000). *Semiotics in Language Education.* Berlin: Mouton de Gruyter.

– *Encyclopedic Dictionary of Semiotics, Media, and Communications.* Toronto: University of Toronto Press.

Danesi, M., and Perron, P. (1999). *Analyzing Cultures.* Bloomington: Indiana University Press.

Dante Alighieri (1957 [1305]). *De vulgari eloquentiae.* Ed. A. Marigo. Florence: Le Monnier.

Darwin, C. (1859). *The Origin of Species.* New York: Collier.

– (1871). *The Descent of Man.* New York: Modern Library.

– (1872). *The Expression of the Emotions in Man and Animals.* London: John Murray.

De Lacy, P.H., and De Lacy, E.A. (1941). *Philodemeus on Methods of Inference.* Philadelphia: American Philological Association.

De Laguna, G.A. (1927). *Speech: Its Function and Development.* Bloomington: Indiana University Press.

Deacon, T.W. (1997). *The Symbolic Species: The Co-Evolution of Language and the Brain.* New York: Norton.

Deely, J. (1980). *The Signifying Animal: The Grammar of Language and Experience.* Bloomington: Indiana University Press.

– (1982). *Introducing Semiotics.* Bloomington: Indiana University Press.

– (1985). Semiotic and the Liberal Arts. *The New Scholasticism* 59: 296–322.

– (1990). *Basics of Semiotics.* Bloomington: Indiana University Press.

Dennett, D.C. (1991). *Consciousness Explained.* Boston: Little, Brown.

Descartes, R. (1637). *Essaies philosophiques.* Leyden: L'imprimerie de Ian Maire.

Douglas, M. (1992). *Objects and Objections.* Toronto: Toronto Semiotic Circle.

Dubois, P. (1988). *L'acte photographique.* Brussels: Labor.

Dunning, W.V. (1991). *Changing Images of Pictorial Space: A History of Visual Illusion in Painting.* Syracuse: Syracuse University Press.

Eccles, J.C. (1979). *The Human Mystery.* New York: Springer.

– (1992). *The Human Psyche.* London: Routledge.

Eco, U. (1972a). *Einführung in die Semiotik.* München: Fink.

– (1972b). Introduction to a Semiotics of Iconic Signs. *VS: Quaderni di Studi Semiotici* 2: 1–15.

– (1976). *A Theory of Semiotics.* Bloomington: Indiana University Press.

– (1977). The Influence of Roman Jakobson on the Development of Semiotics. In *Roman Jakobson: Echoes of His Scholarship,* ed. D. Armstrong and C.H. van Schoonefeld, 39–58. Lisse: Peter de Ridder Press.

– (1980). The Sign Revisited. *Philosophy and Social Criticism* 7: 261–297.

– (1984). *Semiotics and the Philosophy of Language.* Bloomington: Indiana University Press.

Eco, U., and Sebeok, T.A., eds. (1983). *The Sign of Three: Dupin, Holmes, Peirce.* Bloomington: Indiana University Press.

Efron, D. (1972 [1941]). *Gesture, Race, and Culture.* The Hague: Mouton.

Ekman, P. (1985). *Telling Lies.* New York: Norton.

Ekman, P., and Friesen, W. (1969). The Repertoire of Nonverbal Behavior: Categories, Origins, Usage, and Coding. *Semiotica* 1: 49–98.

– (1975). *Unmasking the Face.* Englewood Cliffs, NJ: Prentice-Hall.

Elstein, A.S., et al. (1978). *Medical Problem Solving: An Analysis of Clinical Reasoning.* Cambridge, Mass.: Harvard University Press.

Emerson, A.E. (1938). Termite Nests – A Study of the Phylogeny of Behavior. *Ecological Monographs* 8: 247–284.

Engen, T. (1982). *The Perception of Odours.* New York: Academic.

Engler, R. (1962). Théorie et critique d'un principe saussurien: L'arbitraire du signe. *CFS* 19: 5–66.

Ennion, E.R., and Tinbergen, N. (1967). *Tracks.* Oxford: Oxford University Press.

Erckenbrecht, U. (1976). *Das Geheimnis des Fetischismus Grundmotive der Marxschen Erkenntiskritik.* Frankfurt am Main: Europäische Verlaganstalt.

Fabrega, H. (1974). *Disease and Social Behavior: An Interdisciplinary Perspective.* Cambridge, Mass.: MIT Press.

Feher, M., Naddaf, R., and Tazi, N., eds. (1989). *Fragments for a History of the Human Body.* New York: Zone.

Fillmore, C.J. (1972). A Grammarian Looks at Sociolinguistics. *Georgetown University Monograph Series in Languages and Linguistics* 25: 273–287.

– (1973). May We Come In? *Semiotica* 9: 97–116.

– (1997). *Lectures on Deixis.* Stanford: CSLI Publications.

Fisch, M. (1980). Foreword to *You Know My Method,* ed. T.A. Sebeok and J. Umiker-Sebeok, 7–13. Bloomington: Gaslight Publications.

Fisch, M.H. (1978). Peirce's General Theory of Signs. In *Sight, Sound, and Sense,* ed. T.A. Sebeok, 31–70. Bloomington: Indiana University Press.

Fiske, J.C. (1979). *Introduction to Communication Studies.* London: Methuen.

Fox, J.J. (1975). On Binary Categories and Primary Symbols: Some Rotinese Perspectives. In *The Interpretation of Symbolism,* ed. R. Willis, 99–132. New York: John Wiley and Sons.

Freedman, A.M., Kaplan, H.I., and Sadock, B.J. (1972). *Modern Synopsis of Comprehensive Textbook of Psychiatry.* Baltimore: Williams & Wilkins.

Frege, G. (1892). Über Sinn und Bedeutung. *Zeitschrift für Philologie und philologische Kritik* 100: 25–50.

Frei, H. (1944). Systèmes de déictiques. *AI* 4: 111–129.
– (1950). Zéro, vide et intermittent. *Zeitschrift für Phonologie* 4: 161–191.
French, A.P., and Kennedy, P.J., eds. (1985). *Niels Bohr: A Centenary Volume.* Cambridge, Mass.: Harvard University Press.
Freud, S. (1927). Fetishism. In *The Standard Edition of the Complete Psychological Works* 21, ed. J. Strachey, 149–157.
Friedmann, H. (1955). The Honey-Guides. *U.S. National Museum Bulletin* 208. Washington, DC: Smithsonian.
Frisch, K., von. (1967). *The Dance Language and Orientation of Bees.* Cambridge, Mass.: Harvard University Press.
Frisch, K. von, and Frisch, O. von. (1974). *Animal Architecture.* New York: Harcourt.
Frutiger, A. (1989). *Signs and Symbols.* New York: Van Nostrand.
Furnham, A. (1988). Write and Wrong: The Validity of Graphological Analysis. *The Skeptical Inquirer* 13: 64–69.
Gale, R.M. (1967). Indexical Signs, Egocentric Particulars, and Token-Reflexive Words. *The Encyclopedia of Philosophy* 4: 151–155.
Gardiner, A.H. (1932). *The Theory of Speech and Language.* Oxford: Clarendon Press.
Gardner, B.T., and Gardner, R.A. (1975). Evidence for Sentence Constituents in the Early Utterances of Child and Chimpanzee. *Journal of Experimental Psychology* 104: 244–262.
Gardner, M. (1968). *Logic Machines, Diagrams and Boolean Algebra.* New York: Dover.
Gardner, R.A., and Gardner, B.T. (1969). Teaching Sign Language to Chimpanzees. *Science* 165: 664–672.
Garnier, P. (1896). *Fétischistes: Pervertis et invertis sexuels.* Paris.
Garver, N. (1986). Review of Shapiro 1983. *Transactions of the Charles S. Peirce Society* 22: 68–74.
Gebhard, P.H. (1969). Fetishism and Sadomasochism. *Science and Psychoanalysis* 15: 71–80.
Genette, G. (1988). *Narrative Discourse Revisited.* Ithaca: Cornell University Press.
Geras, N. (1971). Essence and Appearance: Aspects of Fetishism in Marx's *Capital. New Left Review* 65: 69–85.
Gessinger, J., and Rahden, W. von, eds. (1988). *Theorien vom Ursprung der Sprache.* Berlin: Mouton de Gruyter.

Ginzburg, C. (1983). Morelli, Freud and Sherlock Holmes. In *The Sign of Three*, ed. U. Eco and T.A. Sebeok, pp. 81–118. Bloomington: Indiana University Press.

Gipper, H. (1963). *Bausteine zur Sprachinhaltforschung: Neuere Sprachbetrachtung im Austausch mit Geistes- und Naturwissenshcaft.* Düsseldorf: Pädagogischer Verlag Schwann.

Godel, R. (1953). La question des signes zéro. *CFS* 11: 31–41.

Goffman, E. (1959). *The Presentation of Self in Everyday Life.* New York: Anchor.

– (1963). *Stigma: Notes on the Management of Spoiled Identity.* Englewood Cliffs, NJ: Prentice-Hall.

Gombrich, E.H. (1951). Meditations on a Hobby Horse or the Roots of Artistic Form. In *Aspects of Form*, ed. L.L. Whyte, 209–228. Bloomington: Indiana University Press.

Goode, J. (1992). Food. In *Folklore, Cultural Performances, and Popular Entertainments*, ed. R. Bauman, 233–245. Oxford: Oxford University Press.

Goody, J. (1982). *Cooking, Cuisine and Class.* Cambridge: Cambridge University Press.

Gould, S.J., and Vrba, E.S. (1982). Exaptation: A Missing Term in the Science of Form. *Paleobiology* 8: 4–15.

Greenberg, J.H. (1987). *Language in the Americas.* Stanford: Stanford University Press.

Greenbie, B. (1981). *Spaces: Dimensions of the Human Landscape.* New Haven: Yale University Press.

Greimas, A.J. (1987). *On Meaning: Selected Essays in Semiotic Theory*, trans. P. Perron and F. Collins. Minneapolis: University of Minnesota Press.

Greimas, A.J., and Courtés, J. (1979). *Semiotics and Language.* Bloomington: Indiana University Press.

Guthrie, R. Dale. (1976). *Body Hot Spots: The Anatomy of Human Social Organs and Behavior.* New York: Van Nostrand Reinhold.

Haas, W. (1957). Zero in Linguistic Description. *Studies in Linguistic Analysis*, special volume of the Philological Society of London, 35–53. Oxford: Blackwell.

Hadamard, J. (1945). *An Essay on the Psychology of Invention in the Mathematical Field.* Princeton: Princeton University Press.

Haldane, J.B.S. (1955). Animal Communication and the Origin of Human Language. *Science Progress* 43: 385–401.

Hall, E.T. (1966). *The Hidden Dimension*. New York: Doubleday.
– (1973). *The Silent Language*. New York: Anchor.
Hall, K.R.L., and De Vore, I. (1965). Baboon Social Behavior. In *Primate Behavior*, ed. I. Devore, 53–110. New York: Holt, Rinehart and Winston.
Halliday, M.A.K. (1975). *Learning How to Mean: Explorations in the Development of Language*. London: Arnold.
– (1985). *Introduction to Functional Grammar*. London: Arnold.
Haraway, D. (1989). *Primate Visions: Gender, Race and Nature in the World of Modern Science*. London: Routledge.
Hardwick, C.S., ed. (1977). *Semiotic and Significs: The Correspondence between Charles S. Peirce and Victoria Lady Welby*. Bloomington: Indiana University Press.
Harnad, S.R., Steklis, H.B., and Lancaster, J., eds. (1976). *Origins and Evolution of Language and Speech*. New York: New York Academy of Sciences.
Harré, R. (1981). *Great Scientific Experiments*. Oxford: Phaidon Press.
Harrison, P.A. (1983). *Behaving Brazilian: A Comparison of Brazilian and North American Social Behavior*. Rowley, Mass.: Newbury House.
Hawkes, T. (1977). *Structuralism and Semiotics*. Berkeley: University of California Press.
Hearne, V. (1986). *Adam's Task: Calling Animals by Name*. New York: Knopf.
Hediger, H. (1967). Verstehens- und Veständingunsmöglichkeiten zwischen Mensch und Tier. *Schweizerische Zeitschrift für Psychologie und ihre Anwendungen* 26: 234–255.
Hediger, H. (1968). *The Psychology and Behaviour of Animals in Zoos and Circuses*. New York: Dover.
Heidel, W.A. (1941). *Hippocratic Medicine: Its Spirit and Method*. New York: Columbia University Press.
Heisenberg, W. (1949). *The Physical Principles of the Quantum Theory*. New York: Dover.
Herskovits, M. (1948). *Man and His Works*. New York: Alfred A. Knopf.
Hesse, M. (1967). Models and Analogy in Science. *The Encyclopedia of Philosophy* 5: 354–359.
Hewes, G.W. (1973). Primate Communication and the Gestural Origin of Language. *Current Anthropology* 14: 5–24.
– (1974). *Language Origins: A Bibliography*. The Hague: Mouton.

Hinton, H.E. (1973). Natural Deception. In *Illusion in Nature and Art*, ed. R.L. Gregory and E.H. Gombrich, 97–159. London: Duckworth.

Hinton, L., Nichols, J., and Ohala, J.J., eds. (1994). *Sound Symbolism*. Cambridge: Cambridge University Press.

Hjelmslev, L. (1963). *Prolegomena to a Theory of Language*. Madison: University of Wisconsin Press.

Hobbes, T. (1656). *Elements of Philosophy*. London: Molesworth.

Hockett, C.F. (1960). The Origin of Speech. *Scientific American* 203: 88–96.

Hoffmeyer, J. (1996). *Signs of Meaning in the Universe*. Bloomington: Indiana University Press.

Hollander, A. (1978). *Seeing through Clothes*. Harmondsworth: Penguin.

Hollander, J. (1959). The Metrical Emblem. *Kenyon Review* 21: 279–296.

Hudson, L. (1972). *The Cult of the Fact*. New York: Harper & Row.

Humboldt, W. von. (1836 [1988]). *On Language: The Diversity of Human Language-Structure and Its Influence on the Mental Development of Mankind*, trans. P. Heath. Cambridge: Cambridge University Press.

Humphries, W.C. (1968). *Anomalies and Scientific Theories*. San Francisco: Freeman.

Husserl, E. (1970 [1890]). *Philosophie der Arithmetik*, ed. L. Eley. The Hague: Nijhoff.

Huxley, J. (1966). A Discussion of Ritualization of Behaviour in Animals and Men. *Philosophical Transactions of the Royal Society of London* 251: 247–526.

Hymes, D. (1971). *On Communicative Competence*. Philadelphia: University of Pennsylvania Press.

Ingram, D. (1978). Typology and Universals of Personal Pronouns. In *Universals of Human Language*, ed. J.H. Greenberg, 213–247. Stanford: Stanford University Press.

Inhelder, B., and Piaget, J. (1958). *The Growth of Logical Thinking from Childhood through Adolescence*. New York: Basic.

Jackendoff, R. (1994). *Patterns in the Mind: Language and Human Nature*. New York: Basic Books.

Jacob, F. (1974). *The Logic of Living Systems: A History of Heredity*. London: Allen Lane.

– (1982). *The Possible and the Actual*. Seattle: University of Washington Press.

Jakobson, R. (1960). Linguistics and Poetics. In *Style in Language*, ed. T.A. Sebeok, 350–377. New York: John Wiley & Sons.

– (1963 [1957]). *Essais de linguistique générale*. Paris: Éditions de Minuit.

– (1965). Quest for the Essence of Language. *Diogenes* 51: 21–37.

– (1966). Signe zéro. In *Readings in Linguistics* II, ed. E. Hamp et al., 109–115. Chicago: University of Chicago Press.

– (1970). Language in Relation to Other Communication Systems. In *Linguaggi nella società e nella tecnica*, ed. C. Olivetti, 3–16. Milan: Edizioni di Comunità.

– (1971). *Selected Writings II: Word and Language*. The Hague: Mouton.

– (1974). *Main Trends in the Science of Language*. New York: Harper & Row.

– (1980). *The Framework of Language*. Ann Arbor: Michigan Studies in the Humanities.

Jarvella R.H., and Klein, W., eds. (1982). *Speech, Place and Action: Studies in Deictic and Related Topics*. New York: John Wiley and Sons.

Jastrow, J. (1930). *A History of Psychology in Autobiography* 1: 135–162.

– (1930). Joseph Jastrow. Ed. by C. Murchison. *A History of Psychology in Autobiography* 1: 135–162.

Jaynes, J. (1976). *The Origin of Consciousness in the Breakdown of the Bicameral Mind*. Toronto: University of Toronto Press.

Jerne, N.K. (1985). The Generative Grammar of the Immune System. *Science* 229: 1057–1059.

Jespersen, O. (1964). *Language, Its Nature, Development, and Origin*. New York: Norton.

Jhally, S. (1987). *The Codes of Advertising: Fetishism and the Political Economy of Meaning in the Consumer Society*. New York: St Martin's Press.

Johnson, S. (1979). Nonverbal Communication in the Teaching of Foreign Languages. PhD dissertation, Indiana University.

Johnson-Laird, P.N. (1983). *Mental Models*. Cambridge, Mass.: Harvard University Press.

Kahn, T.C. (1969). Symbols and Man's Nature. *The International Journal of Symbolology* 1: 5–6.

Kant, I. (1790). *Critique of Judgment*. New York: Hafner Press.

Kantor, J.R. (1936). *An Objective Psychology of Grammar*. Bloomington: Indiana University Press.

Kecskemeti, P. (1952). *Meaning, Communication, and Value.* Chicago: University of Chicago Press.

Kendon, A. (1991). Some Considerations for a Theory of Language Origins. *Man* 26: 199–221.

Kevles, D.J. (1985). *In the Name of Eugenics: Genetics and the Uses of Human Heredity.* New York: Alfred A. Knopf.

Kinsey, A.C., Pomeroy, W.B., Marshall, C.E., and Gebhard, P.H. (1953). *Sexual Behavior in the Human Female.* Philadelphia: Saunders.

Kinzle, D. (1982). *Fashion and Fetishism: A Social History of the Corset, Tight-Lacing and Other Forms of Body-Sculpture in the West.* Totowa, NJ: Rowman and Littlefield.

Kleinpaul, R. (1972 [1888]). *Sprache ohne Worte: Idee einer allgemeinen Wissenschaft der Sprache.* The Hague: Mouton.

Kloft, W. (1959). Versuch einer Analyse der Trophobiotischen Beziehungen von Ameisen zu Aphiden, *Biologische Zentralblatt* 78: 863–870.

Koch, W.A. (1986). *Philosophie der Philologie und Semiotik.* Bochum: Brockmeyer.

Koch, W.A., ed. (1989). *Geneses of Language.* Bochum: Brockmeyer.

Köhler, W. (1925). *The Mentality of Apes.* London: Routledge and Kegan Paul.

Konner, M. (1987). On Human Nature: Love among the Robots. *The Sciences* 27: 14–23.

– (1991). Human Nature and Culture: Biology and the Residue of Uniqueness. in *The Boundaries of Humanity,* ed. J.J. Sheehan and M. Sosna, 103–124. Berkeley: University of California Press.

Kosslyn, S.M. (1983). *Ghosts in the Mind's Machine: Creating and Using Images in the Brain.* New York: W.W. Norton.

Krafft-Ebing, R. von. (1886). *Psychopathia sexualis.* Stuttgart.

Krampen, M. (1981). Phytosemiotics. *Semiotica* 36: 187–209.

– (1991). *Children's Drawings: Iconic Coding of the Environment.* New York: Plenum.

Kuhn, C.G. (1821–1833). *Claudii Galeni opera omnia.* Leipzig: Cnobloch.

Kuhn, T.S. (1970). *The Structure of Scientific Revolutions.* Chicago: University of Chicago Press.

Labov, W., and Fanshel, D. (1977). *Therapeutic Discourse: Psychotherapy as Conversation.* New York: Academic.

Laitman, J.T. (1983). The Evolution of the Hominid Upper Respiratory System and Implications for the Origins of Speech. In *Glossogenetics: The Origin and Evolution of Language*, ed. E. de Grolier, 63–90. Utrecht: Harwood.

Laitman, J.T. (1990). Tracing the Origins of Human Speech. In *Anthropology: Contemporary Perspectives*, ed. P. Whitten and D.E.K. Hunter, 124–130. Glenview, Ill.: Scott, Foresman and Co.

Lambert, J.H. (1764). *Semiotik oder Lehre von der Bezeichnung der Gedanken und Dinge*. Leipzig: Johann Wendler.

Landar, H. (1966). *Language and Culture*. Oxford: Oxford University Press.

Landsberg, M.E., ed. (1988). *The Genesis of Language: A Different Judgement of Evidence*. Berlin: Mouton.

Langer, S. (1948). *Philosophy in a New Key*. Cambridge: Harvard University Press.

– (1957). *Problems of Art*. New York: Scribner's.

Larker, M., ed. (1968). *Bibliographie zur Symbolik, Ikonographie und Mythologie*. Baden-Baden: Heitz.

Latham, R.G. (1848). *The Works of Thomas Sydenham, M.D.* London: Sydenham Society.

Lausberg, H. (1960). *Handbuch der Literarischen Theorik*. Munich: Max Huber.

Lawick-Goodall, J. (1968). The Behaviour of Free-Living Chimpanzees in the Gombe Stream Reserve. *Animal Behaviour Monographs* 1: part 3.

Lawrence, C. (1982). Illnesses and Their Meanings. *Times Literary Supplement*, 1 October, 148.

Leach, E. (1976). *Culture and Communication*. Cambridge: Cambridge University Press.

Leech, G. (1981). *Semantics: The Study of Meaning*. Harmondsworth: Penguin.

Leitch, T.M. (1986). *What Stories Are: Narrative Theory and Interpretation*. University Park: Pennsylvania State University Press.

Lekomcev, J.K. (1977). Foundations of General Semiotics. In *Soviet Semiotics*, ed. D.P. Lucid, 39–44. Baltimore: Johns Hopkins University Press.

Lenneberg, E. (1967). *The Biological Foundations of Language*. New York: John Wiley.

Levelt, W.J.M. (1989). *Speaking: From Intention to Articulation*. Cambridge, Mass.: MIT Press.

Lévi-Strauss, C. (1958). *Anthropologie structurale*. Paris: Librairie Plon.

– (1962). *Le totémisme aujourd'hui*. Paris: Presses Universitaires de France.

– (1964). *The Raw and the Cooked*. London: Cape.

Lewis, C.I. (1946). *An Analysis of Knowledge and Valuation*. LaSalle, Ill.: Open Court.

Leyhausen, P. (1967). Biologie von Ausdruck und Eindruck. *Psychologische Forschung* 31: 177–227.

Lieberman, P. (1972). *The Speech of Primates*. The Hague: Mouton.

– (1975). *On the Origins of Language*. New York: Macmillan.

– (1984). *The Biology and Evolution of Language*. Cambridge, Mass.: Harvard University Press.

– (1991). *Uniquely Human: The Evolution of Speech, Thought, and Selfless Behavior*. Cambridge, Mass.: Harvard University Press.

Liebman, R., Minuchin, S., and Baker, L. (1974a). An Integrated Program for Anorexia Nervosa. *American Journal of Psychiatry* 131: 432–435.

– (1974b). The Role of Family in the Treatment of Anorexia Nervosa. *Journal of the Academy of Child Psychology* 3: 264–274.

Linden, E. (1986). *Silent Partners: The Legacy of the Ape Language Experiments*. New York: Signet.

Liszka, J.J. (1989). *The Semiotic Study of Myth: A Critical Study of the Symbol*. Bloomington: Indiana University Press.

Lloyd, J.E. (1966). *Studies on the Flash Communication System in Photinus Fireflies*. Ann Arbor: Museum of Zoology, University of Michigan.

Locke, J. (1690 [1975]). *An Essay Concerning Human Understanding*. Ed. P.H. Nidditch. Oxford: Clarendon.

Lorenz, K. (1952), *King Solomon's Ring*. New York: Crowell.

– (1971). *Studies in Animal and Human Behaviour*. Cambridge, Mass.: Harvard University Press.

Lotman, J. (1984). O Semiosfere. *Trudy po znakovym sistemam* 17: 5–623.

Lotman, J., and Uspenskij, B.A. (1978). On the Semiotic Mechanism of Culture. *New Literary History* 9: 211–232.

Lotman, J., and Uspenskij, B.A., eds. (1973). *Ricerche semiotiche*. Torino: Einaudi.

Lotman, J.M. (1977). Primary and Secondary Communication Modeling

Systems. In *Soviet Semiotics*, ed. P. Lucid, 95–98. Baltimore: Johns Hopkins University Press.

Lott, D.F., and Sommer, R. (1967). Seating Arrangements and Status. *Journal of Personality and Social Psychology* 7: 90–94.

Lucid, D.P., ed. (1977). *Soviet Semiotics: An Anthology.* Baltimore: Johns Hopkins University Press.

Lucy, J.A. (1992). *Language Diversity and Thought: A Reformulation of the Linguistic Relativity Hypothesis.* Cambridge: Cambridge University Press.

Luria, A.R. (1970). *Traumatic Aphasia.* New York: Humanities Press.

Lyons, J. (1977). *Semantics.* Cambridge: Cambridge University Press.

Mackay, A.L. (1984). The Code Breakers. *The Sciences* 24: 13–14.

Majno, G. (1975). *The Healing Hand.* Cambridge, Mass.: Harvard University Press.

Mallory, J.P. (1989). *In Search of the Indo-Europeans: Language, Archaeology and Myth.* London: Thames and Hudson.

Malson, L. (1973). Un entretien avec Claude Lévi-Strauss. *Le Monde* 20: 3–5.

Maritain, J. (1943). *Sign and Symbol: Redeeming the Time.* London: Geoffrey Bles.

– (1957). Language and the Theory of Sign. In *Language: An Enquiry into Its Meaning and Function*, ed. R. Nanda Anshen, 86–101. New York: Harper & Brothers.

Markus, R.A. (1957). St. Augustine on Signs. *Phronesis* 2: 60–83.

McBryde, C.M., and Backlow, R.S. (1970). *Signs and Symptoms: Applied Pathologic Physiology and Clinical Interpretation.* Philadelphia: Lippincott.

McKean, K. (1982). Diagnosis by Computer. *Discovery* 3: 62–65.

McLennan, J.F. (1869). The Worship of Animals and Plants. *Fortnightly Review* 12: 407–427, 562–582.

McNeill, D. (1987). *Psycholinguistics: A New Approach.* New York: Harper & Row.

– (1992). *Hand and Mind: What Gestures Reveal about Thought.* Chicago: University of Chicago Press.

Meiland, J.W. (1970). *The Nature of Intention.* London: Methuen.

Melzack, R. (1972). The Perception of Pain, in *Physiological Psychology*, ed. R.F. Thompson, 223–231. San Francisco: Freeman.

– (1988). Pain. In *A Lexicon of Psychology, Psychiatry and Psychoanalysis*, ed. J. Kuper, 288–291. London: Routledge.

Metz, C. (1974). *Film Language: A Semiotics of the Cinema*. Oxford: Oxford University Press.

– (1985). Photography and Fetish. *October* 34: 81–90.

Miller, G.A., and Gildea, P.M. (1991). How Children Learn Words. In *The Emergence of Language: Development and Evolution*, ed. W.S.-Y. Wang, 150–158. New York: W.H. Freeman.

Miller, J. (1978). *The Body in Question*. New York: Random House.

Moenssens, A.A. (1971). *Fingerprint Techniques*. Philadelphia: Chilton.

Money, J. (1986). *Lovemaps: Clinical Concepts of Sexual/Erotic Health and Pathology, Paraphilia, and Gender Identity from Conception to Maturity*. Baltimore: Johns Hopkins University Press.

Morgan, C.L. (1895). *Introduction to Comparative Psychology*. London: Scott.

Morris, C.W. (1938). *Foundations of the Theory of Signs*. Chicago: University of Chicago Press.

– (1946). *Signs, Language and Behavior*. Englewood Cliffs, NJ: Prentice-Hall.

– (1971). *Writings on the General Theory of Signs*. The Hague: Mouton.

Morris, D. (1969). *The Human Zoo*. New York: McGraw-Hill.

– (1994). *The Human Animal*. London: BBC Books.

Morris, D., et al. (1979). *Gestures: Their Origins and Distributions*. London: Cape.

Mortenson, J. (1987). *Whale Song and Wasp Maps: The Mystery of Animal Thinking*. New York: Dutton.

Mounin, G. (1981). Sémiologie médicale et sémiologie linguistique. *Confrontations Psychiatriques* 19: 43–58.

Mounin, G. 1970. *Introduction à la sémiologie*. Paris: Les Éditions de Minuit.

Müller, F.M. (1861). *Lectures on the Science of Language*. London: Longmans.

Munn, N.D. (1973). *Walbiri Iconography: Graphic Representation and Cultural Symbolism in a Central Australian Society*. Ithaca: Cornell University Press.

Nadin, M., and Zakia, R.D. (1994). Creating Effective Advertising Using Semiotics. New York: Consultant Press.

Nespoulous, J.L., Perron, P., and Lecours, A.R., eds. (1986). *The Biological Foundations of Gestures: Motor and Semiotic Aspects*. Hillsdale, NJ: Lawrence Erlbaum.

Neuburger, M. (1906). *Geschichte der Medezin*. Stuttgart: Enke.

Noiré, L. (1917). *The Origin and Philosophy of Language*. Chicago: Open Court.

Nöth, W. (1985). *Handbuch der Semiotik*. Stuttgart: J.B. Metzlersche Verlagsbuchhandlung.

Nöth, W. (1990). *Handbook of Semiotics*. Bloomington: Indiana University Press.

Ogden, C.K., and Richards, I.A. (1923). *The Meaning of Meaning*. New York: Harcourt, Brace.

Ong, Walter J. (1977). *Interfaces of the Word: Studies in the Evolution of Consciousness and Culture*. Ithaca: Cornell University Press.

Opie, I., and Opie, P. (1959). *The Lore and Language of Schoolchildren*. Frogmore, SC: Paladin.

Osgood, C.E., and Sebeok, T.A., eds. (1954). *Psycholinguistics: A Survey of Theory and Research Problems*. Bloomington: Indiana University Press.

Osgood, C.E., and Suci, G.E. (1953). Factor Analysis of Meaning. *Journal of Experimental Psychology* 49: 325–328.

Osgood, C.E., Suci, G.J., and Tannenbaum, P.H. (1957). *The Measurement of Meaning*. Urbana: University of Illinois Press.

Osolsobé, I. (1979). On Ostensive Communication. *Studia Semiotyczne* 9: 63–75.

Ostwald, P.F. (1968). Symptoms, Diagnosis and Concepts of Disease: Some Comments on the Semiotics of Patient-Physician Communication. *SocSeil* 7: 95–106.

Paget, R. (1930). *Human Speech*. London: Kegan Paul.

Paine, R., and Sherman, W. (1970). Arterial Hypertension. In *Signs and Symptoms*, ed. C.M. Macbryde and R.S. Backlow, 45–56. Philadelphia: Lippincott.

Patterson, F.G. (1978). The Gestures of a Gorilla: Language Acquisition in Another Pongid. *Brain and Language* 5: 72–97.

Patterson, F.G. and Linden, E. (1981). *The Education of Koko*. New York: Holt, Rinehart and Winston.

Pavlov, I. (1902). *The Work of Digestive Glands*. London: Griffin.

Pazukhin, R. (1972). The Concept of Signal. *Lingua Posn*. 16: 25–43.

Pedersen, H. (1931). *The Discovery of Language*. Bloomington: Indiana University Press.

Peirce, C.S. (1868). Some Consequences of Four Incapabilities. *Journal of Speculative Philosophy* 2: 140–151.

– (1935–66). *Collected Papers*. Ed. C. Hartshorne, P. Weiss, and A.W. Burks. Cambridge, Mass.: Harvard University Press.

Phillips, E.D. (1973). *Greek Medicine.* London: Thames and Hudson.

Piaget, J. (1969). *The Child's Conception of the World.* Totowa, NJ: Littlefield, Adams & Co.

Piaget, J., and Inhelder, J. (1969). *The Psychology of the Child.* New York: Basic Books.

Pike, K. (1967). *Language in Relation to a Unified Theory of the Structure of Human Behavior.* The Hague: Mouton.

Pitts, W., and McCulloch, W.S. (1947). How We Know Universals: The Perception of Auditory and Visual Forms. *Bulletin of Mathematical Biophysics* 9: 127–149.

Pohl, J. (1968). *Symboles et langages.* Paris: Sodi.

Polunin, I. (1977). The Body as an Indicator of Health and Disease. In *The Anthropology of the Body,* ed. J. Blacking, 34–56. London: Academic.

Popper, K. (1972). *Objective Knowledge: An Evolutionary Approach.* Oxford: Clarendon.

– (1976). *The Unending Quest.* Glasgow: Harper Collins.

Popper, K., and Eccles, J. (1977). *The Self and the Brain.* Berlin: Springer.

Premack, A. (1976). *Why Chimps Can Read.* New York: Harper and Row.

Premack, D., and Premack, A.J. (1983). *The Mind of an Ape.* New York: Norton.

Preziosi, D. (1979). *The Semiotics of the Built Environment: An Introduction to Architectonic Analysis.* Bloomington: Indiana University Press.

– (1989). *Rethinking Art History: Meditations on a Coy Science.* New Haven: Yale University Press.

Prieto, L.J. (1975). Études de linguistique et de sémiologie générales. Geneva: Librairie Droz.

Prince, G. (1982). *Narratology: The Form and Functioning of Narrative.* Berlin: Mouton.

Prodi, G. (1981). Sintomo/diagnosi. *Ricerca-Socializzazione* 12: 972–992.

Propp, V.J. (1928). *Morphology of the Folktale.* Austin: University of Texas Press.

Putnam, H. (1973). Meaning and Reference. *The Journal of Philosophy* 70: 699–711.

Raffler-Engel, W. von, Wind, J., and Jonker, A., eds. (1989). *Studies in Language Origins.* Amsterdam: John Benjamins.

Ransdell, J. (1986). Index. *Encyclopedic Dictionary of Semiotics* 1: 340–341.

Rector, M., and Trinta, A.R. (1985). *Comunicação não verbal: A gestualidade Brazileira*. Petropolis: Editor Vozes.

Reichenbach, H. (1948). *Elements of Symbolic Logic*. New York: Macmillan.

Révész, G. (1956). *The Origins and Prehistory of Language*. New York: Philosophical Library.

Revzina, O.G. (1972). The Fourth Summer School on Secondary Modeling Systems. *Semiotica* 6: 222–243.

Richards, I.A. (1936). *The Philosophy of Rhetoric*. Oxford: Oxford University Press.

– (1969). Tipi e campioni. *Strumenti Critici* 3: 187–193.

Roberts, D. (1973). *The Existential Graphs of Charles S. Peirce*. The Hague: Mouton.

Rohter, L. (1932). Macabre Relic Is Laid to Rest by Mexicans. *New York Times*, 10 December, 9.

Roiphe, H. (1973). The Infantile Fetish. *Psychoanalytic Study of the Child* 28: 147–166.

Rosch, E. (1973a). On the Internal Structure of Perceptual and Semantic Categories, in *Cognitive Development and Acquisition of Language*, ed. T.E. Moore, 111–144. New York: Academic.

– (1973b). Natural Categories. *Cognitive Psychology* 4, 328–350.

Ross, S. (1998). *What Gardens Mean*. London: University of Chicago Press.

Rousseau, J.J. (1966). *Essay on the Origin of Language*. Trans. J.H. Moran and A. Gode. Chicago: University of Chicago Press.

Rowell, T. (1972). *The Social Behaviour of Monkeys*. Harmondsworth: Penguin.

Royce, A.P. (1977). *The Anthropology of Dance*. Bloomington: Indiana University Press.

Rudy, S. (1986). Semiotics in the U.S.S.R. In *The Semiotic Sphere*, ed. T.A. Sebeok and J. Umiker-Sebeok, chapter 25. New York: Plenum.

Ruesch, J. (1972). *Semiotic Approaches to Human Relations*. The Hague: Mouton.

Ruesch, J., and Kees, W. (1956). *Nonverbal Communication: Notes on the Visual Perception of Human Relations*. Berkeley: University of California Press.

Rumbaugh, D.M. (1977). *Language Learning by Chimpanzee: The Lana Project*. New York: Academic.

Russell, B. (1940). *An Inquiry into Meaning and Truth,* London: Allen and Unwin.

Saint-Martin, F. (1990). *Semiotics of Visual Language.* Bloomington: Indiana University Press.

Sakitt, B. (1975). Locus of Short-Term Visual Storage. *Science* 190: 1318–1319.

Sanders, G. (1970). Peirce's Sixty-Six Signs? *Transactions of the Charles S. Peirce Society* 6: 3–16.

Sapir, E. (1921). *Language.* New York: Harcourt, Brace, and World.

– (1929). The Status of Linguistics as a Science. *Language* 5: 207–214.

– (1931). Communication. *Encyclopedia of the Social Sciences* 4: 78–481.

Sarton, G. (1954). *Galen of Pergamon.* Lawrence: University of Kansas Press.

Saussure, F. de (1916). *Cours de linguistique générale.* Paris: Payot.

Savage-Rumbaugh, E.S., Rumbaugh, D.M., and Boysen, S.L. (1978). Symbolic Communication between Two Chimpanzees. *Science* 201: 641–644.

Savan, D. (1983). Toward a Refutation of Semiotic Idealism. *Semiotic Inquiry* 3: 1–8.

Sayers, D.L. (1932). *Have His Carcase.* New York: Harcourt, Brace and Co.

Schiffman, N. (1997). *Abracadabra! Secret Methods Magicians and Others Use to Deceive Their Audience.* Amherst: Prometheus Books.

Schindler, W. (1953). A Case of Crutch Fetishism as the Result of a Literal Oedipus Complex. *International Journal of Sexology* 6: 131–135.

Schleidt, M. (1980). Personal Odor and Nonverbal Communication. *Ethology and Sociobiology* 1: 225–231.

Schmandt-Besserat, D. (1978). The Earliest Precursor of Writing. *Scientific American* 238: 50–59.

– (1989). Two Precursors of Writing: Plain and Complex Tokens. In *The Origins of Writing,* ed. W.M. Senner, 27–40. Lincoln: University of Nebraska Press.

– (1992). *Before Writing.* 2 vols. Austin: University of Texas Press.

Schneirla, T.C. (1965). Aspects of Stimulation and Organization in Approach/Withdrawal Processes Underlying Vertebrate Behavioral Development. *Advances in the Study of Behavior* 1: 1–74.

Scholes, R. (1982). *Semiotics and Interpretation.* New Haven: Yale University Press.

Schor, N. (1985). Female Fetishism: The Case of George Sand. *Poetics Today* 6: 301–310.

Schuller, G. (1997). *The Compleat Conductor.* London: Oxford University Press.

Sebeok, T.A. (1963a). Communication among Social Bees; Porpoises and Sonar; Man and Dolphin. *Language* 39: 448–466.

– (1963b). Communication in Animals and Men. *Language* 39: 448–466.

– (1968). *Animal Communication: Techniques of Study and Results of Research.* Bloomington: Indiana University Press.

– (1972a). *Perspectives in Zoosemiotics.* The Hague: Mouton.

– (1972b). Problems in the Classification of Signs. In *Studies for Einar Haugen*, 511–521. The Hague: Mouton.

– (1973a). Semiotics: A Survey of the State of the Art. In *Current Trends in Linguistics* 12, ed. T.A. Sebeok, 161–213. The Hague: Mouton.

– (1973b). Semiotica e affini. *VS: Quaderni di Studi Semiotici* 3: 1–11.

– (1976). *Contributions to the Doctrine of Signs.* Lisse: Peter de Ridder Press.

– (1979). *The Sign and Its Masters.* Austin: University of Texas Press.

– (1981a). *The Play of Musement.* Bloomington: Indiana University Press.

– (1981b). Karl Bühler. In *Die Welt als Zeichen: Klassiker der modernen Semiotik*, ed. M. Krampen et al., 34–46. Berlin: Severin und Siedler.

– (1985). *Contributions to the Doctrine of Signs.* Lanham, Md.: University Press of America.

– (1986). *I Think I Am a Verb.* New York: Plenum.

– (1989). Fetish. *American Journal of Semiotics* 6: 51–65.

– (1990). *Essays in Zoosemiotics.* Toronto: Toronto Semiotic Circle.

– (1991a). *Semiotics in the United States: The View from the Center.* Bloomington: Indiana University Press.

– (1991b). *A Sign Is Just a Sign.* Bloomington: Indiana University Press.

– (2001). *Global Semiotics.* Bloomington: Indiana University Press.

Sebeok, T.A., and Danesi, M. (2000). *The Forms of Meaning: Modeling Systems Theory and Semiotics.* Berlin: Mouton de Gruyter.

Sebeok, T.A., and Umiker-Sebeok, J., eds. (1992). *Biosemiotics.* Berlin: Mouton de Gruyter.

Shands, H.C. (1970). *Semiotic Approaches to Psychiatry.* The Hague: Mouton.

Shannon, C.E., and Weaver, W. (1949). *The Mathematical Theory of Communication.* Urbana: University of Illinois Press.

Shapiro, M. (1983). *The Sense of Grammar: Language as Semeiotic.* Bloomington: Indiana University Press.

Sherzer, J. (1973). Verbal and Nonverbal Deixis: The Pointed Lip Gesture among the San Blas Cuna. *Language in Society* 2: 117–131.

Shevoroshkin, V., ed. (1989). *Reconstructing Languages and Cultures.* Bochum: Brockmeyer.

Short, T.L. (1982). Life among the Legisigns. *Transactions of the Charles S. Peirce Society* 18: 285–310.

Siegel, R.E. (1973). *Galen on Psychology, Psychopathology, and Function and Diseases of the Nervous System.* Basel: Karger.

Skinner, B.F. (1938). *The Behavior of Organisms.* New York: Appleton-Century-Crofts.

Skousen, R. (1989). *Analogical Modeling of Language.* Dordrecht: Kluwer.

Smith, C.G. (1985). *Ancestral Voices: Language and the Evolution of Human Consciousness.* Englewood Cliffs, NJ: Prentice-Hall.

Smith, J.W. (1977). *The Behavior of Communicating: An Ethological Approach.* Cambridge, Mass.: Harvard University Press.

Smith, W.J. (1965). Message, Meaning, and Context in Ethology. *The American Naturalist* 99: 405–409.

– (1969a). Displays and Messages in Intraspecific Communication. *Semiotica* 1: 357–369.

– (1969b). Messages of Vertebrate Communication. *Science* 165: 145–150.

Sonea, S., and Panisset, M. (1983). *A New Bacteriology.* Boston: Jones and Bartlett.

Sonesson, G. (1989). *Pictorial Concepts: Inquiries into the Semiotic Heritage and Its Relevance for the Analysis of the Visual World.* Lund: Lund University Press.

Sontag, S. (1978). *Illness as Metaphor.* New York: Farrar, Straus & Giroux.

Sørensen, H.S. (1963). *The Meaning of Proper Names.* Copenhagen: Gad.

Sperling, M. (1963). Fetishism in Children. *Psychoanalytic Quarterly* 32: 374–392.

Spang-Hanssen, H. (1954). Recent Theories on the Nature of the Language Sign. *Travaux du Cercle Linguistique de Copenhague,* vol. 9.

Staal, J.F. (1971). What Was Left of Pragmatism in Jerusalem. *Language Sciences* 14: 29–32.

Staehlin, W. (1914). Zür Psychologie und Statistike der Metapherm. *Archiv für Gesamte Psychologie* 31, 299–425.

Stahl, S. (1989). *Literary Folkloristics and the Personal Narrative.* Bloomington: Indiana University Press.

Staiano, K.V. (1979). A Semiotic Definition of Illness. *Semiotica* 28: 107–125.

– (1982). Medical Semiotics: Redefining an Ancient Craft. *Semiotica* 38: 319–346.

Stamp Dawkins, M. (1993). *The Search for Animal Consciousness.* Oxford: Freeman.

Stanosz, B. (1970). Formal Theories of Extension and Intension of Expressions. *Semiotica* 2: 102–114.

Stewart, A.H. (1976). *Graphic Representation of Models in Linguistic Theory.* Bloomington: Indiana University Press.

Stewart, I. (1975). The Seven Elementary Catastrophes. *New Scientist* 68: 447–454.

Stratton, J. (1987). *The Virgin Text: Fiction, Sexuality, and Ideology.* Norman: University of Oklahoma Press.

Stross, B. (1976). *The Origin and Evolution of Language.* Dubuque, Iowa: W.C. Brown.

Sturtevant, E.H. (1947). *An Introduction to Linguistic Science.* New Haven: Yale University Press.

Swadesh, M. (1951). Diffusional Cumulation and Archaic Residue as Historical Explanations. *Southwestern Journal of Anthropology* 7: 1–21.

– (1959). Linguistics as an Instrument of Prehistory. *Southwestern Journal of Anthropology* 15: 20–35.

– (1971). *The Origins and Diversification of Language.* Chicago: Aldine-Atherton.

Telegdi, Z. (1976). Zur Herausbildung des Begriffs 'sprachliches Zeichen' und zur stoischen Sprachlehre. *Acta Linguistica Scientiarum Hungaricae* 26: 267–305.

Tembrock, G. (1971). *Biokommunication: Informationsbetragung im biologischen Bereich.* Berlin: Akademie-Verlag.

Temkin, O. (1973). *Galenism.* Ithaca: Cornell University Press.

Terrace, H.S. (1979). *Nim.* New York: Knopf.

Thibaud, P. (1975). *La logique de Charles Sanders Peirce: De l'algèbre aux graphes.* Aix-en-Provence: Université de Provence.

Thom, R. (1973). De l'icône au symbole: Esquisse d'une théorie du symbolisme. *Cahiers Internationaux de Symbolisme* 22–23: 85–106.

- (1974). La linguistique, discipline morphologique exemplaire. *Critique* 30: 235–245.
- (1975). *Structural Stability and Morphogenesis: An Outline of a General Theory of Models.* Reading: W.A. Benjamin.
- (1980). L'espace et les signes. *Semiotica* 38: 205–215.

Thorndyke, E.L. (1898/1911). *Animal Intelligence.* New York: Macmillan.

Thorpe, W.H. (1961). *Bird-song.* Cambridge: Cambridge University Press.
- (1967). Vocal Imitation and Antiphonal Song and Its Implications. In *Proceedings of the XIV International Ornithological Congress*, ed. D.W. Snow, 245–263. Oxford: Blackwell.

Tinbergen, N. (1963). On Aims and Methods of Ethology. *Zeitschrift für Tierpsychologie* 20: 410–433.

Tinbergen, N., and Perdeck, A.C. (1950). On the Stimulus Situation Releasing the Begging Response in the Newly Hatched Herring Gull Chick. *Behaviour* 3: 1–39.

Todorov, T. (1973). Semiotics. *Screen* 14: 15–23.

Toller, S. van, and Donn, G.H., eds. (1989). *Perfumery: The Psychology and Biology of Fragrance.* New York: Routledge, Chapman and Hall.

Toolan, M.J. (1988). *Narrative: A Critical Linguistic Introduction.* London: Routledge.

Trabant, J. (1981). *Die Welt als Zeichen. Klassiker der modernen Semiotik.* Berlin: Severin and Siedler.

Trevarthen, C. (1989). Signs before Speech. In *The Semiotic Web 1988*, ed. T.A. Sebeok and J. Umiker-Sebeok, 689–755. Berlin: Mouton de Gruyter.

Trevarthen, C. (1990). Signs before Speech. In *The Semiotic Web 1989*, ed. T.A. Sebeok and Jean Umiker-Sebeok, Pp. 689–755. Berlin: Mouton de Gruyter.

Tsuda, A. (1984). *Sales Talk in Japan and the United States. An Ethnographic Analysis of Contrastive Speech Events.* Washington DC: Georgetown University Press.

Tulving, E. (1972). Episodic and Semantic Memory. In *Organization of Memory*, ed. E. Tulving and W. Donaldson, 23–46. New York: Academic.

Uexküll, J. von. (1909). *Umwelt und Innenwelt der Tiere.* Berlin: Springer.
- (1973 [1928]). *Theoretische Biologie.* Frankfurt: Suhrkamp.

- (1982a). The Theory of Meaning. *Semiotica* 42: 1–87.
- (1982b). Semiotics and Medicine. *Semiotica* 38: 205–215.
- (1989). Jakob von Uexküll's Umwelt-Theory. In *The Semiotic Web 1988*, ed. T.A. Sebeok and J. Umiker-Sebeok, 129–158. Berlin: Mouton de Gruyter.

Uexküll, T. von, ed. (1981). *Kompositionslehre der Natur: Biologie als undogmatische Naturwissenschaft by Jakob von Uexküll*. Frankfurt am Main: Verlag Ullstein (Propylaen).

Uexküll, T. von, et al. (1979). *Lehrbuch der Psychosomatischen Medizin*. Munich: Urban & Schwarzenberg.

Uexküll, T. von, et al. (1993). Endosemiotics. *Semiotica* 96: 5–51.

Ullmann, S. (1951). *Principles of Semantics*. Glasgow: Jackson, Son & Co.

Valesio, P. (1969). Icons and Patterns in the Structure of Language. *AC Acts of the International Congress of Linguistics II* [Bucharest] 10: 383–387.

Van Wing, R.P.J. (1938). *Études bakongo II, Religion et magie*. Brussels: G. van Campenhout.

Vigener, G. (1989). Dieser Schuch ist kein Schuch – Zur Semiotik des Fetischs. In *Semiotik der Geschlechter Akten des 6. Symposiums der österreichischen Gesellschaft für Semiotik, Salzburg 1987*, ed. J. Bernard, T. Klugsberger, and G. Wiltham, 341–352. Stuttgart: Heinz.

Vygotsky, L.S. (1962). *Thought and Language*. Cambridge, Mass.: MIT Press.

Wallis, M. (1973). On Iconic Signs. In *Recherches sur les systèmes signifiants*, ed. J. Rey-Debove, 481–498. The Hague: Mouton.

Walther, E. (1984). Die Beziehung zwischen Semiotik und Linguistik. *Semiotica* 52: 111–117.

Ward, L., and Raffler-Engel, W. von. (1980). The Impact of Nonverbal Behavior on Foreign Language Teaching. In *Aspects of Nonverbal Communication*, ed. W. von Raffler-Engel, 287–304. Lisse: Swets and Zeitlinger.

Watson, J.B. (1929). *Psychology from the Standpoint of a Behaviorist*. Philadelphia: Lippincott.

Waugh, L.R. (1982). Marked and Unmarked: A Choice between Unequals in Semiotic Structure. *Semiotica* 38: 299–318.

Way, E.C. (1991). *Knowledge Representation and Metaphor*. Dordrecht: Kluwer.

Weckler, W. (1973). *The Sexual Code*. New York: Anchor.

Weimann, W. (1962). Über Tatowierungsfetischismus. *Archiv für Kriminologie* 130: 106–109.

Weinreich, U. (1968). Semantics and Semiotics. *International Encyclopedia of the Social Sciences* 14: 164–69.

Weiss, P., and Burks, A. (1945). Peirce's Sixty-Six Signs. *Journal of Philosophy* 42: 383–388.

Wells, G. (1986). *The Meaning Makers: Children Learning Language and Using Language to Learn.* Portsmouth: Heinemann.

Wells, R. (1954). Meaning and Use. *Word* 10: 235–250.

– (1967). Distinctively Human Semiotic. *Social Science Information* 6: 103–124.

Welte, W. (1974). *Moderne Linguistik.* Munich: Max Hüber.

Werner, H., and Kaplan, B. (1963). *Symbol Formation: An Organismic-Developmental Approach to the Psychology of Language and the Expression of Thought.* New York: John Wiley.

Wertheimer, M. (1923). Untersuchungen zur Lehre von der Gestalt, II. *Psychologische Forschungen* 4: 301–350.

Wescott, R.W. (1971). Linguistic Iconism. *Language* 47: 416–428.

Wescott, R.W., ed. (1974). *Language Origins.* Silver Springs, Md.: Linstok Press.

Wheeler, J.A. (1988). World as System Self-Synthesized by Quantum Networking. *IBM Journal of Research and Development* 32: 1–15.

Wheelwright, P. (1954). *The Burning Fountain: A Study in the Language of Symbolism.* Bloomington: Indiana University Press.

White, L.A. (1940). The Symbol: The Origin and Basis of Human Behavior. *Philosophy of Science* 7: 451–463.

Whorf, B.L. (1956). *Language, Thought, and Reality.* Ed. J.B. Carroll. Cambridge, Mass.: MIT Press.

Wickler, W. (1968). *Mimicry in Plants and Animals.* New York: McGraw Hill.

Wiener, N. (1949). *Cybernetics, or Control and Communication in the Animal and the Machine.* Cambridge, Mass.: MIT Press.

Wierzbicka, A. (1996). *Semantics: Primes and Universals.* Oxford: Oxford University Press.

Wilder, H.H., and Wentworth, B. (1918). *Personal Identification.* Boston: Badger.

Wills, D.D. (1990). Indexifiers in Wolof. *Semiotica* 78: 193–218.

Wilson, C. (1989). *The Misfits: A Study of Sexual Outsiders.* London: Carroll and Graf.

Wilson, E.O. (1971). The Prospects for a Unified Sociobiology. *American Scientist* 59: 400–403.

– (1975). *Sociobiology: The New Synthesis.* Cambridge, Mass.: Harvard University Press.

– (1979). *On Human Nature.* New York: Bantam.

– (1984). *Biophilia.* Cambridge, Mass.: Harvard University Press.

Wimsatt, W.R. (1954). *The Verbal Icon: Studies in the Meaning of Poetry.* New York: University of Kentucky Press.

Wintsch, S. (1979). The Vocabulary of Gestures: Nonverbal Communication in Foreign Languages. *Research & Creative Activity* 3: 6–11.

Yerkes, R. (1916). *The Mental Life of Monkeys and Apes.* New Haven: Yale University Press.

Zavitzianos, G. (1971). Fetishism and Exhibitionism in the Female and Their Relationship to Psychopathy and Kleptomania. *International Journal of Psycho-Analysis* 52: 297–305.

Zeman, J.J. (1964). The Graphical Logic of C.S. Peirce. Dissertation, University of Chicago.

Index